BEN HUR

by Patrick Barlow

SAMUEL FRENCH

samuelfrench.co.uk

FOR AMATEUR PRODUCTION ENQUIRIES

UNITED KINGDOM AND WORLD
EXCLUDING NORTH AMERICA
plays@samuelfrench.co.uk
020 7255 4302/01

Each title is subject to availability from Samuel French,
depending upon country of performance.

Cover artwork and design SWD

THINKING ABOUT PERFORMING A SHOW?

There are thousands of plays and musicals available to perform from Samuel French right now, and applying for a licence is easier and more affordable than you might think

---

From classic plays to brand new musicals, from monologues to epic dramas, there are shows for everyone.

Plays and musicals are protected by copyright law so if you want to perform them, the first thing you'll need is a licence. This simple process helps support the playwright by ensuring they get paid for their work, and means that you'll have the documents you need to stage the show in public.

Not all our shows are available to perform all the time, so it's important to check and apply for a licence before you start rehearsals or commit to doing the show.

LEARN MORE & FIND THOUSANDS OF SHOWS

Browse our full range of plays and musicals and find out more about how to license a show
www.samuelfrench.co.uk/perform

Talk to the friendly experts in our Licensing team for advice on choosing a show, and help with licensing
plays@samuelfrench.co.uk   020 7387 9373

Acting Editions

BORN TO PERFORM

Playscripts designed from the ground up to work the way you do in rehearsal, performance and study

---

Larger, clearer text for easier reading

Wider margins for notes

Performance features such as character and props lists, sound and lighting cues, and more

---

+ CHOOSE A SIZE AND STYLE TO SUIT YOU

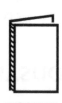

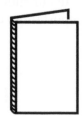

STANDARD EDITION

Our regular paperback book at our regular size

SPIRAL-BOUND EDITION

The same size as the Standard Edition, but with a sturdy, easy-to-fold, easy-to-hold spiral-bound spine

LARGE EDITION

A4 size and spiral bound, with larger text and a blank page for notes opposite every page of text. Perfect for technical and directing use

---

LEARN MORE **samuelfrench.co.uk/actingeditions**

ABOUT PATRICK BARLOW

Besides his version of Lew Wallace's *Ben Hur*, Patrick's Olivier-nominated adaptation of *A Christmas Carol* has played off-Broadway and London's West End while his 4-person adaptation of *The 39 Steps* has played in over forty countries world-wide, winning Olivier, Helpmann, Moliere and Tony Awards and making Patrick the most performed playwright in America for 2012/13. Most recently his re-writing of John Milton's *Comus* has played to critical acclaim at Shakespeare's Globe Theatre.

Patrick is also celebrated in the UK for his two-man theatre company National Theatre of Brent, whose comedy epics include *Wagner's Ring Cycle*, *The Charles and Diana Story*, *The Messiah*, *The Wonder of Sex*, *The Arts and How They Was Done*, *The Black Hole of Calcutta*, *The Life and Times of the Dalai Lama* and *Zulu!* They have won two Sony Gold Awards, a Premier Ondas Award for Best European Comedy and the New York Festival Gold Award for Best Comedy.

Other screenwriting includes *Van Gogh* (Prix Futura Berlin Film Festival), *Revolution!!* (Best Comedy Jerusalem Film Festival) and the BAFTA-winning *The Young Visiters*. Publications include *Shakespeare: The Truth!* and *The Complete History of the Whole World*. Patrick has also appeared in *Absolutely Fabulous*, *Shakespeare in Love*, *Notting Hill*, *Nanny McPhee* and *Bridget Jones's Diary*. He is currently writing theatre versions of *The Hound of the Baskervilles* and *Dracula*.

AUTHOR'S PREFACE

This is a play of two worlds. The world of Daniel's play, adapted from Lew Wallace's celebrated nineteenth century tome *Ben Hur* and the world of Daniel's company – The Daniel Veil Theatre Collective who are battling the odds to put the play on. It is the clash of these two worlds, the colossal grandiosity of one and the over-eager paucity of the other, that gives the play its story, its tension and – particularly – its comedy. But – and this is the crucial part – comedy though it certainly is – no one, director, writer, designer, choreographer and particularly actors, should *know* they're in a comedy.

In other words, the whole show, for it to work, must be performed, designed, written, with the utmost seriousness. No "jokes" in other words, nothing signalled. Daniel and his company must perform the *Ben Hur* characters as if they are performing Shakespeare or Aeschylus or Racine. And in full classical style. However loopy and convoluted and pretentious the writing, Daniel (who we must believe wrote it) doesn't *know* it's loopy or convoluted or pretentious. He *believes* he is an artist of classical or biblical stature. The same goes for his portrayal of the title role which, to his mind, is on a par with an Olivier or Cumberbatch. All the actors should have the same inner and intense confidence and deadly certainty of purpose. Partly because they are playing deadly serious actors, but the characters they are playing take themselves deadly seriously too.

The great Buster Keaton said, with comedy, the more seriously the actors, writer, director, take it, the funnier it is. Watch Keaton facing the ludicrous and impossible odds of *The General* or *The Navigator* or *Steamboat Bill Junior*. Or Stan Laurel solemnly putting his whole life into moving a crated piano across a gorge chased by a gorilla in *The Music Box*. Even though these films are funny and Keaton and Laurel do wildly hilarious things, they never even suggest (however beautifully choreographed the routines) that they have any idea they're funny. They are right inside the situation they are playing. They don't show us where to laugh. Life is deadly serious for the silent comedians. They don't know it's funny. So it is for the *Ben Hur* characters and the Daniel Veil characters who live their lives in constant fear of disaster.

If Daniel and his company stumble over lines like: *"There is no other path now but mine own path whereon I now must on I now must now I in I on I tread on,"* the problem for them is that both text and delivery (and memorizing lines) are really beyond their abilities but more importantly that anything that "goes wrong", any little stumble, is just the tiniest hiccough and fazes no one for a moment, so sure is their confidence.

Most important, if something *does* go wrong, the lines go askew, the plume of a helmet gets stuck in a door, a pillar collapses, Crystal and Omar are caught kissing, they *keep going*, even when Daniel nearly doesn't keep going, they keep going because they convince themselves *the audience won't have noticed.* A dangerous misbelief shared by many actors but, however misguided, it can carry them through virtually any stage adversity. In *Ben Hur*, it even carries them through the increasing crisis moments in Act Two, even the end of Act Two when everything threatens to explode. The audience haven't noticed. That's what keeps them going. Even at the end, after nearly losing two actors, after blowing up two chariots, after sins are openly confessed, they reach their triumphant end and resurrection in the full belief nothing was noticed. That they got away with it.

On the point of things going wrong, please note that I have used "sotto" or "hisses" many times as a stage direction or even "very shocked and muted". The point is the painful and emotional arguments that increasingly proliferate between Daniel and his actors are not to be signaled, not to be cheapened for comic effect. The point is these moments – as I've said earlier – must be REAL. Played for real, played for truth. In other words, the question that needs asking is what would REALLY happen if an actor lost his temper, felt sudden deep despair, nearly killed another actor? My point is they would cover it up, hide it and convince themselves the audience was none the wiser.

Even the mis-spellings and mis-pronunciations and convoluted grammar and garbled mock-classical language should be played faithfully and justified by the actors who, not having read the original book, assume that's how it should be. There need be no jokes, repeat, no jokes for their own sake. Every line in the script must be justified or explained. They should be explored through rehearsal and improvisation. Lines like "unstable chicken", for example. I don't think Daniel wrote this. I think Edgar thinks of it on the spur of the moment but, whatever the reason, it needs exploring properly and playing truthfully. There's no excuse for a funny line that is just there for its own sake. Everything must have a reason and be justified. So if Edgar did just think of the unstable chicken line spontaneously, it shouldn't cause a lot of shocked looks and mugging by the actors. They cover it up, hide it, convince themselves the audience never spotted it and carry on.

A final note. When the Daniel Veil story collides with or invades the Ben Hur story, when they switch between their real characters and their play characters in the same scene, I include stage directions to make this clear, eg:
This is uncomfortably close to the recent situation. But it is a rehearsed scene and they have to continue. Messala laughs cruelly and disappears.

When they flip characters, I will change character names, mid-scene. So JUDAH might address ESTHER, then change to DANIEL then address CRYSTAL etc. I hope this is clear to follow and makes sense of the two stories as they gradually, and slowly but surely nudge, tangle, invade and finally downright explode in each other's worlds. But don't worry.

The audience won't even notice.

Patrick Barlow – November 2016

**Other plays by PATRICK BARLOW
published and licensed by Samuel French**

A Christmas Carol

The 39 Steps

**FIND PERFECT PLAYS TO PERFORM AT
www.samuelfrench.co.uk/perform**

MUSIC USE NOTE

Licensees are solely responsible for obtaining formal written permission from copyright owners to use copyrighted music in the performance of this play and are strongly cautioned to do so. If no such permission is obtained by the licensee, then the licensee must use only original music that the licensee owns and controls. Licensees are solely responsible and liable for all music clearances and shall indemnify the copyright owners of the play(s) and their licensing agent, Samuel French, against any costs, expenses, losses and liabilities arising from the use of music by licensees. Please contact the appropriate music licensing authority in your territory for the rights to any incidental music.

IMPORTANT BILLING AND CREDIT REQUIREMENTS

If you have obtained performance rights to this title, please refer to your licensing agreement for important billing and credit requirements.

BEN HUR was first presented at the Watermill Theatre, in association with Fiery Angel, in 2012 and directed by Sean Foley and Patrick Barlow. This latest version was presented at the Tricycle Theatre, in association with Fiery Angel and Fiery Dragons, in 2015 with the following cast and creative team:

DANIEL/JUDAH BEN HUR – John Hopkins

OMAR/MESSALA/JESUS – Ben Jones

CRYSTAL/TIRZAH/ESTHER/MARY– Alix Dunmore

EDGAR/SARAH/QUINTUS ARRIUS – Richard Durden

Director – Tim Carroll
Designer – Michael Taylor
Lighting Designer – Mark Doubleday
Sound Designers – Ben & Max Ringham
Movement Director – Siân Williams
Costume Supervisor – Catherine Kodicek
Backstage Crew – Simon Sinfield, Elizabeth Patrick, Caitlin O'Reilly, Jessica Bishop and Kate Riedler

AUTHOR'S ACKNOWLEDGEMENTS

There are many people to thank for the magnificent support this
play has received in its (so far) two UK productions:
Edward Snape, Marilyn Eardley, Jon Bath, Sarah Sweeney,
Hugh de la Bédoyère, Nick Morrison, and Rachel Francis at
Fiery Angel.
Hedda Beeby and the team at the Watermill Theatre.
Indhu Rubasingham, Bridget Kalloushi, Trish McElhill, Jennifer
Bakst and Shaz McGee at the Tricycle Theatre.
My agent Jane Villiers and her team at Sayle Screen.
Thanks also to Tamara Harvey, John Manning and Briony
Barnett and epic thanks to my spectacular assistant Phoebe
Eclair-Powell.

FOR
SAM JOE NELL
who are always there, always get the point and never cease to wonder

CHARACTERS

DANIEL VEIL – 30
JUDAH BEN HUR –30
MELCHIOR – 70-100
NUBIAN DANCER – 18

CRYSTAL SINGER – 25
MARY – 20-50
TIRZAH – 16
ESTHER – 24
ANCIENT SLAVE – 100
NUBIAN DANCER 2 – 18
CATALINYA – 20
NABOTH - 16
MRS PILATE – 40

OMAR LORD – 30
MESSALA – 30
JESUS – 30
CASPAR – 70-100
ARCHANGEL GABRIEL – 30
GALLEY CAPTAIN – 50
ROMAN CAPTAIN – 30
GALLEY SLAVE 3 – 20
NUBIAN DANCER 3 – 18
VALENTINYO – 20

EDGAR T CHESTERFIELD – 70
BALTHASAR – 70-100
SARAH – 60
CENTURION/SLAVE-DRIVER – 50
QUINTUS ARRIUS – 60-70
PONTIUS PILATE – 60-70

SETTING

Ancient Rome, Jerusalem, Syrian Desert, Nazareth,
Mediterranean Sea.

TIME: AD 1-30 and Modern Day

The set should be practical for the needs of the production
but should reflect Daniel Veil's desire to recreate as
authentic a representation of Jerusalem and Rome in the
1st century AD as is possible within his somewhat limited
means.

Any music used should be nothing short of epic in nature.

As per the author's note on the nature of this piece – all
set, props, musical interludes etc must be used and played
entirely seriously.

ACT ONE

1 Auditorium.

Music: overture.

DANIEL *(voiceover)* Good evening and welcome to the Tricycle Theatre and tonight's play. The world premiere of Ben Hur – A Tale of the Christ, presented by the Daniel Veil Theatre Collective, and adapted, directed, designed and choreographed by Daniel Veil. But before we begin tonight's performance please be certain to turn off all mobile telephones and any photographic equipment. Thank you. And now – to introduce tonight's performance – please welcome myself. Daniel Veil.

Enter DANIEL.

Thank you. Thank you so much. And welcome to Ben Hur – A Tale of the Christ. Adapted by myself from the great American novel written in 1880 by the American general and American Civil War general General Lewis or Lew Wallace. Tonight we will be recreating for you every scene of his entire nine-hundred-page novel, including an authentic Roman sea battle, a lifelike reconstruction of ancient Rome and of course the world-famous and iconic chariot race. But not only that. I am also thrilled to announce that for the first time in the history of epic theatre, every one of the seventy thousand historically accurate and psychologically complex characters of Ben Hur – A Tale of the Christ – will be played by a cast of four. Thank you. And featuring –

Music.

Enter OMAR.

No no Omar!

Exit OMAR.

– myself Daniel Veil in the title – or leading – role of Ben Hur.

Music.

Thank you. Thank you so much. Thank you. So now lets meet the Daniel Veil Theatre Collective. And – first but by no means least – an up-and-coming young actor and highly popular, so I gather, with Welsh daytime TV audiences and playing the villain Messala – Omar Lord.

Music.

Enter OMAR. *He bows.*

Secondly – taking on many of the crucial older and more – older roles, renowned Shakespearean actor and Radio Four favourite – he has come out of retirement especially for us and very much against his doctor's orders – Edgar T Chesterfield.

Music.

Enter EDGAR. *He bows.*

And finally – it is my truly enormous pleasure to introduce a very special and may I say unique young talent. She is, in my personal opinion, one of the brightest, not to say hottest, young stars of tomorrow. As soon as I met her I knew I had no option but to cast her as my captivating young lover Esther – Crystal Singer.

Music.

Enter CRYSTAL. *She bows.*

As a collective there's not much we don't know about each other and I'm sure it's no secret that I've become rather – fond of Crystal during rehearsal. And – well – I have reason to believe the feeling might be mutual. But who knows? Let's just say – watch this space.

He kisses her hand. CRYSTAL *smiles awkwardly.*

Thank you Crystal. And the Daniel Veil Theatre Collective. Thank you so much. But just before we begin, I'd like to just say that tonight's show is a very special show for me personally because a certain member of my family is in tonight. At least I hope so.

Looks shyly up at the gallery.

I'll say no more for the moment. So – on with the show! The world premiere performance of Ben Hur – A Tale of the Christ by General Lew Wallace adapted by Daniel Veil. But first –

Music.

– before we raise the curtain, we are now going to attempt something never before ever attempted in this or, I believe, any other theatre. As we part the veils of history –

The mists of time fill the stage. Exit OMAR, CRYSTAL *and* EDGAR. *They disappear through the smoke.* EDGAR *gets lost but is guided out by* CRYSTAL.

– and witness the actual summoning up of General Lew himself, who, albeit long deceased, returneth now in person, to begin our tale.

Music.

Exit DANIEL *through the smoke.*

Enter EDGAR *as* GENERAL LEW. *He has only just got into an American Civil War uniform and Abe Lincoln beard. He carries a leather-bound book.*

GENERAL LEW Well howdy there. And yes indeed it is myself. General Lewis or Lew Wallace himself, who findeth himself transported through the mists of time to introduce this, dare I humbly say, mighty work of mine, as was just mentioned. But who is this Ben Hur? And why a tale of the Christ? And – more to the point – how come a nineteenth century American Civil War American general, who never once in his life hadst opened a single book, didst write a nine hundred and forty-eight-page novel set in the distant epoch of ancient Roman times, about which he knoweth precisely nothing? How didst all this thing come to pass, how was this endless book writ I hear you cry? Sadly the answer to that great mystery is still unknown – even to myself. And so now without let or hindrance or just impediment let us now begin our mighty endless tale.

He opens the book.

Music: *mystic cymbal clash.*

The Story of Ben Hur. A Tale of the Christ. By me. Chapter one. Page –

He turns several pages.

– page – page – page – page – one.

Music.

And lo. One ancient night long ago on an ancient road, worn by the winds of time, in the great Syrian desert of El-Jebel-akh-Lebel, three travellers did happenstance to meet. All three from the – four corners of the earth doth come – majestically bestridetheth are they upon their proud vessels. Their ships of the desert.

Sound effects: camel bark.

Searching, ever searching for what they know not what they what of. I leave thee now in their ancient company.

GENERAL LEW *exits through the mists of time. He coughs a bit.*

Music *builds.*

2 Syrian Crossroads. Night.

Enter on camels, DANIEL *as* MELCHIOR, OMAR *as* CASPAR, *doing a majestic choreographed camel-sway. They gaze intently up into the night sky. They see each other and stop.*

Manoeuver their camels to face each other. They bow.

CASPAR All hail o stranger.

MELCHIOR All hail also o stranger.

Sound effects: camel bark.

CASPAR But see. Another stranger.

They look offstage, they wait.

Sound effects: camel barks.

MELCHIOR See where he cometh!

CASPAR Yes!

MELCHIOR Nearly here.

Sound effects: camel barks.

Enter EDGAR *as* BALTHASAR. *A little flustered as he has only just got out of his* GENERAL LEW *costume. He manoeuvers his camel to face the others. They all bow.*

BALTHASAR All hail o strangers!

CASPAR Hail!

MELCHIOR Hail!

BALTHASAR Tell me strangers, wouldst thou be – wise men?

MELCHIOR A wise man am I.

CASPAR And I a wise man also.

BALTHASAR In that case we are – three wise men!

Sound effects: three camels bark.

MELCHIOR Melchior am I.

CASPAR I Caspar am.

BALTHASAR And I am Balthasar am.

MELCHIOR But what strange coincidence is this that we three kings of Orient are met here? All searching – for a sign!

CASPAR Will we ever find it?

BALTHASAR Or has our journey proved in vain?

Music.

MELCHIOR But list! What is that?

He looks up.

Look! Look!

They all look at him.

Not at me! There! Look up there!

They all look up. Gasp!

Light effects: a bright light shines down.

CASPAR 'Tis a star!

MELCHIOR Star of wonder!

CASPAR Star of light!

BALTHASAR Like a tiger in the night!

MELCHIOR But see! See where it shineth! Upon a simple human humble stable there! Ride brethren ride!

The stable comes on. The **WISE MEN** *gallop on the spot. The stable squeaks into position.*

Look! Here it is.

CASPAR Further than we thought.

They stop galloping. Look at the stable.

BALTHASAR Let us step forth and open this simple human humble simple stumble human...dumbledor!

*The three **WISE MEN** open the stable. Reveal **MARY** in her blue robe, holding the new-born baby.*

MELCHIOR But look!

Sound effects: baby cry.

CASPAR A little baby! All in swaddling is he swaddled! Surely a little tiny little baby cannot be the end of all our searching.

MARY Hello.

BALTHASAR Hello.

MELCHIOR Hello.

BALTHASAR Hello.

CASPAR But what ist this tiny little tiny baby might we ask?

MARY A most wondrous tiny baby methinks. But then perhaps I would say that. Being his mother.

*She chuckles ruefully. The **WISE MEN** chuckle too.*

Even so, wonders already hath he performed in his tiny tiny life. Why e'en now – albeit newly born, his little new-born eye didst fall upon a little lame chicken in the stable.

BALTHASAR An un-stable chicken.

MARY Indeed. And immediately didst stretch forth his little tiny hand and – lo! He healed him.

BALTHASAR Healed the chicken?!

*The **WISE MEN** gasp in amazement.*

MELCHIOR Madame –

Sound effects: baby cry.

Madame – we hast searchest day and night to bring gifts
unto your little tiny little tiny baby. For why we know not
or for what purpose who canst tell, but they are thine.

The WISE MEN *awkwardly manoeuvre their camels into
a kneeling position and present their gifts. They are
wrapped up like Christmas presents. One might be a
little Christmas stocking.*

MARY Thank you o three wise men.

BALTHASAR No dear lady. Unblemished as the snow, as spotless
as – as the lark. Thank YOU.

The WISE MEN *pay homage to the baby.* OMAR
surreptitiously goes behind the stable.

Music.

MELCHIOR *(suddenly anxious)* What is that?

BALTHASAR What?

MELCHIOR Canst not hear it?

BALTHASAR Yes! What?

MELCHIOR Someone is here. Some other presence.

BALTHASAR We've given our presents.

MELCHIOR No. NO! But look!

OMAR *appears as the* ARCHANGEL GABRIEL. *With
white unwieldy wings. The* WISE MEN *and* MARY *gasp,
shielding their eyes.*

Aggghh! Art thou – an angel?

GABRIEL AN ARCHANGEL! Behold!

WISE MEN Yes?

GABRIEL You must leave this place!

BALTHASAR But we only just got here.

GABRIEL No no no! Listen! Listen! Dost not hear THAT?!

Sound effects: hurricane wind. Military sounds. Helicopters. Marching men.

Soldiers! Soldiers in the night! Coming for the baby! Take flight! Take flight! Quick! Take the baby from the stable. Do not hang about! The wicked of the earth doth rise! Hide the baby! Hide the baby from the men who would kill him!

Music: builds.

WISE MEN *and* **MARY** *perform a choreographed escaping from the soldiers routine. Smoke fills the stage. The* **WISE MEN** *escape one way,* **MARY** *and the baby escape the other. She waves goodbye and thank you to the* **WISE MEN.** *They disappear into the smoke.* **OMAR,** *still in his wings, is left to heft off the stable. This is easier said than done.*

Music.

Enter **GENERAL LEW.** *The smoke swirls round him.*

GENERAL LEW And so we turn to the next chapter of this mighty tome and lo! Time hath fleeted by a further twenty-five years. But what world now is it that awaits us? Doth Herod the king still rule? Nay, for Herod the king is gone and a new tyrant come. A tyrant without mercy who rules the whole world. Dread Caesar emperor of the Romans. But 'tis not the din of his mighty Roman capital of Rome that doth greet our senses for the next chapter of our tale but the capital of his most mutinous province of Judea. The capital named – Jerusalem!

Sound effects: the distant roar of Jerusalem. People shouting, donkeys, bicycles, car horns, snatches of cafe music. A distant muezzin.

The Jerusalem dawn skyline appears. Minarets and domes. One of the minarets sways. **DANIEL** *nips on and steadies it.*

That once-proud and historic city now crushed and enchained, her bitter weeping people enslaved in their teeming alleyways and back streets by their heartless Roman overlords who know not the name of peace or forgiveness. But not amidst those teeming alleyways and back streets doth our story now continue, but in a mighty and resplendent house. Built high above that weeping people and oblivious to their pain. The name of that mighty house, the House of Hur. Home of the new prince of Hur, Judah Ben Hur.

Music.

3 House of Hur. Day.

TIRZAH BEN HUR runs on. **JUDAH***'s sister. Fifteen years old.*

TIRZAH Mother! Mother! Mother! Mother!

SARA **BEN HUR** *enters. Played by* **EDGAR**. *A Jewish matron in robe and headdress.*

SARA What is it daughter? What is it?

TIRZAH Oh Mother Mother! I can barely believe it Mother!

Falls into her mother's arms.

HE is coming home! Messala! Messala!

Music.

After five whole years! Oh will he come soon do you think?

She runs to the parapet. Leans over.

Sound effects: the roar of Jerusalem.

SARA Tirzah Tirzah!

TIRZAH *runs back.*

Sound effects: cuts.

TIRZAH Yes Mother?

SARA Do be careful my daughter! Do remember the dangerously loose terracotta tile on the ancient ornamental parapet!

TIRZAH Sorry Mother! But o Mother dost think Messala who lived with us for so many years as son and brother will he have changed do you think? After five whole years in the Roman army?

SARA Changed my darling? No no I'm –

Her brow furrows with anxiety.

– sure he wont!

TIRZAH But mother will he – *(gasps!)* I CAN – I CAN BARELY
SAY IT! Will he – propose do you suppose?

SARA *(gasps!)* Propose?! Who knows? Darling daughter don't
get carried away I beg of thee! He is after all your brother
my darling!

TIRZAH But only my adopted brother Mother! Thou didst not
bear him in thine womb!

SARA *(gasps with shock)* Tirzah! Contain thy language I beg
of thee!

TIRZAH O Mother forgive me for mine outspoken speaking!
But let us not forget how Messala didst comest amongst
us. How my father, alas no more, the enormously powerful,
famously rich and mighty merchant Hur, Obadiah Hur, didst
spottest him in the street one day, a starving little beggar
boy with nothing to call his own, not even tiny shoes upon
his tiny starving feet, and taking pity upon him, as was his
wont, bringest him unto our homely home the House of
Hur to live with us and be childhood companion unto me
and my brother –

Takes a breath.

– Judah. Judah Ben Hur.

Music.

O Mother Mother! Do you remember Mother? How they
would laugh and play? And race their little homemade
wooden chariots? Messala and Judah! What was it they
cried out? Down Eros! Up Mars! What happy times were
they, were they not Mother? O Mother Mother will we have
happy times again?

Music. cuts.

SARA Sorry my darling. I was miles away. But – talking of
Judah –

TIRZAH Yes?

SARA Where is Judah?

TIRZAH Judah? Why I believe he is in the gumnasium Mother. Working out.

SARA Working out what?

TIRZAH *(she laughs)* Oh Mother! Tis a modern term oft uséd by the youth. It means –

Music: trumpet call.

But – *(gasps!)* listen! Is that not – *(gasps!)* the tribune's trumpet?

TIRZAH *runs to the parapet. Leans over excitedly. Gasps!*

Sound effects: roar of Jerusalem etc.

SARA Tirzah Tirzah!

TIRZAH *runs back.*

Sound effects: cuts.

TIRZAH Tis he Mother tis he!

SARA What did I just tell you about that dangerously loose ornamental tile on the exotic ornamental terracotta parapet?!

TIRZAH But I saw him Mother! You should see his enormous helmet! I feel quite faint!

SARA I've asked Judah to see to that parapet but does he do anything!? Plainly not! He spends his days in the gumnasium. Buggering up. Your –

TIRZAH Buffing up.

SARA Buffing up. Your father would have fixed that tile! He was a true man. As I am forced to remind your brother on a more or less daily basis!

TIRZAH Mother? Forgive me for saying so Mother but might it not be somewhat psychologically ill-advised to compare a young man negatively with his father on a more or less daily basis? Might it not lead to certain complicated Oedipal issues in later life?

SARA I'm afraid that's all rather Greek to me my darling.

Sound: knocking on door.

(Tizrah and Sarah freeze) Ahhh!

TIRZAH Tis he mother! Tis he! At the front door!

SARA Quick! Where is Esther?

TIRZAH Esther?

SARA Esther. Our beautiful dutiful traditional Jewish serving girl. But also our friend in many respects. Has she finished preparing the lunch she was preparing?

Sound: knocking on door.

Tell her to hurry daughter hurry!

TIRZAH *(calls off)* Esther Esther! Hurry with the lunch!

SARA Quickly!

TIRZAH *(very fast)* Esther Esther! Hurry with the lunch!

TIRZAH *exits.*

ESTHER *(offstage)* Coming mistress!

TIRZAH *re-enters.*

TIRZAH She says it's coming.

SARA Has she done the falafels?

TIRZAH *exits.*

TIRZAH *(offstage)* Have you done the falafels?

ESTHER *(offstage)* Yes.

TIRZAH *re-enters.*

TIRZAH Yes.

Music: trumpet call.

The door opens dramatically. MESSALA *stands there in breastplate and helmet.* TIRZAH *gasps! With painful memory and sudden burgeoning adolescent desire.*

Music:

MESSALA Tirzah.

TIRZAH Messala.

MESSALA You have – grown.

TIRZAH Have I?

MESSALA So fair thou wast, now fairer now thou art than thou wast when thou wert.

Awkward moment.

TIRZAH Thank you.

MESSALA *(bashes breastplate)* Lady Hur.

SARA Messala, no formalities I beg of thee. Call me – Mother!

MESSALA Mother indeed! How could I forget? And – *(looks around emotionally)* the House of Hur! How could I forget that either? Also? Anyway –

TIRZAH 'Tis still your home Messala.

MESSALA Thank you. I was sorry to hear about – Lord Hur.

SARA Obadiah.

MESSALA Was he?

SARA His name.

MESSALA Of course.

SARA Twas was a peaceful end.

MESSALA Most glad am I to hear it. So now there is a new lord here Hur now? New Hur lord here now?

SARA Sorry?

MESSALA A new Hur here lord new here Hur now lord near here –

SARA *(no idea)* Indeed.

MESSALA So – will the new Lord Hur here be – joining us?

Pause.

VOICE Yes Messala. He will.

> MESSALA, TIRZAH, SARA *turn.* JUDAH BEN HUR *appears in a shaft of light. They all gasp! at his charisma.*

Music:

MESSALA Judah Ben Hur

JUDAH Messala Sextus Messala.

MESSALA It has been a long time Judah.

JUDAH It certainly has Messala. How are you?

MESSALA Not bad – thank you. And you?

JUDAH I must not grumble.

MESSALA I am glad to hear it.

JUDAH Likewise.

> *Awkward moment.* TIRZAH *can contain herself no longer.*

TIRZAH O do you remember? Do you? Racing in your little homemade wooden chariots? Getting under Mother's feet? You two boys!

> *They all laugh at the memory.*

MESSALA How could we forget Tirzah?

TIRZAH *(gazing at* MESSALA*)* I didn't forget.

A noticeable look between **CRYSTAL** *and* **OMAR**. **DANIEL** *doesn't notice.*

MESSALA Down Eros!

JUDAH Up Mars!

They fall into each other's arms. They pull away laughing loudly. They fall into each other's arms again, but this time **TIRZAH** *joins them.*

TIRZAH Down Eros!

Another moment between **CRYSTAL** *and* **OMAR**. *They turn away awkwardly.* **OMAR** *becomes* **MESSALA** *again and hugs* **JUDAH**.

MESSALA Up Mars!

JUDAH *looks at* **MESSALA** *and pulls away. They all laugh again even louder before disentangling themselves.*

So anyway Judah how is this wretched country of yours while I've been away? Still the same?

He marches to the parapet. Looks down into the street.

Sound effects: roar of Jerusalem etc.

He nearly leans on the parapet, then marches back.

Sound effects: cuts.

Still the most miserable mutinous province in the empire? With all its riots and rebellions and angels and prophesies and wise men and carpenters and all that miracle-mongering mumbo jumbo! Or has this miserable people of yours finally seen the light?!

JUDAH Light?

MESSALA The light of the world Judah! The light of Rome!

Gives the imperial salute.

Hail Caesar! Oh Judah Judah!

JUDAH What?

MESSALA Just think!

JUDAH What?

MESSALA What we can do!

JUDAH Who?

MESSALA You and me of course! When I've moved back in.

TIRZAH Oh yes! Will you?! Can he Mother?!

MESSALA Slightly bigger room than before I think.

Laughs.

TIRZAH *(laughs)* Yes yes! A much bigger room! He can, can't he Mother?

SARA Um – but of course. Lovely!

MESSALA Judah?

JUDAH Um – lovely!

MESSALA You don't seem very sure.

JUDAH Of course! Ha ha ha! Of course I'm sure!

MESSALA Ha ha ha! Of course you are! The House of Hur can be our home again!

JUDAH Yes!

TIRZAH *YES!*

MESSALA And *(emphatically)* My Headquarters!

JUDAH Your Headquarters?

MESSALA *(more emphatically)* My Headquarters! The new headquarters of the personal tribune to the new Roman governor of Jerusalem.

JUDAH New head – personal – Roman – um –

MESSALA Must I spell it out as if to a child?! Ha ha ha! The new personal tribune to the new Roman governor of Jerusalem? Is – ME!

JUDAH, TIRZAH and **SARA** YOU?!

MESSALA O Judah Judah Judah! Everything is changed now! Remember how we lived in this house as brothers! As youths! But now we are no longer youths! We have put away our youthful things! Now we have a greater purpose! We shall live in this house again!

TIRZAH Yes!

MESSALA But this time – as servants of Rome! And together we shall keep an eye – and spy – on this rebellious mutinous race of yours!

JUDAH Spy? I?

As it dawns.

I SPY?!

MESSALA While all the time living as Romans live! The Roman sandal clad upon our feet, eating decadent Roman dinners by the light of a thousand Roman candles, bathing in the imperial baths with the finest Imperial Leather.

JUDAH *pulls away.*

Music:

O Judah Judah! Let not thy fevered brow be so besmited with anxiety after so tender and brief a reunion! Hast all thy childhood memories departed thee so suddenly? Hast thou forgotten what we were to one another?

JUDAH I – I – I –

An awkward moment. **TIRZAH** *looks bewildered.*

SARA Tirzah my darling?

TIRZAH Yes Mother?

SARA Why not put on your lovely new pretty frock to show Messala?

TIRZAH My lovely new pretty lovely frock? Shall I Messala?

MESSALA Why not?

SARA Then lunch I think.

MESSALA Lunch! Splendid!

SARA Tell Esther to hurry with the lunch while you're fetching the frock.

TIRZAH Certainly Mother.

MESSALA And most fetching will she look in my opinion.

This line is not in DANIEL's *play.* OMAR *had it up his sleeve and slipped it in. Everyone is thrown.*

TIRZAH Right. Shan't – be long Messala.

MESSALA Okay.

Another awkward moment. Possibly a tiny look between DANIEL *and* OMAR. TIRZAH *skips out.*

TIRZAH *(offstage)* Esther Esther?!

ESTHER *(offstage)* Yes young mistress?

TIRZAH *(offstage)* Hurry hurry with the lunch!

ESTHER *(offstage)* Lunch young mistress? Coming right up young mistress.

Sound effects: loud clattering of pots and pans. This goes on quite a long time.

DANIEL, OMAR *and* EDGAR *wait while the clattering goes on. The clattering stops and* CRYSTAL *enters as* ESTHER. ESTHER *is a beautiful servant girl. She carries an exotic tray of food.*

Music:

DANIEL *gazes at the girl of his dreams.*

Luncheon madame.

SARA Thank you Esther –

ESTHER Stuffed grape leaves, grilled fish, Persian cucumbers, bitter tsatsiki, hummus, small chicken shish and...falafels.

SARA You remember Esther, Messala?

MESSALA Yes I remember Esther.

ESTHER Hello Messala. You were once a boy. Now you are a – man.

MESSALA I beg your pardon? Thou durst not speakst unto me in this intimate manner! For now I am your master!

ESTHER Master?!

MESSALA You are a slave are you not?

JUDAH Not a slave Messala! This is Esther!

SARA You grew up with her Messala!

MESSALA A slave I say! They are ALL slaves!

Shouts across the parapet.

All of you!!! Born into this wretched little filthy province.

He turns and smiles.

Not you of course Judah! Or dear Mother. Or sweet Tirzah. You never never never never never shall be slaves! But THEY are slaves! And SHE is a slave! What are you girl?!

ESTHER *stares at him, smouldering.*

Sorry!? What was that?!

ESTHER *smoulders even more. Their faces are very close. They gaze into each other's eyes.*

Slave?! Was that what you said? That's what you said, wasn't it? Slave! My slave! And your slave too Judah!

JUDAH My slave?! No no! Esther's not my –

MESSALA Come on Judah! Don't tell me you care about HER! About THEM! Living their pathetic little pointless lives! Praying for their pathetic little pointless Messiah! You've never even noticed them! All you ever cared about was *yourself* Judah! Gallivanting in the gumnasium! Like a boy! But now – all that's changed! Now you must be a man! For men must rule! Oh Judah! Judah!

Clasps his arms Roman style.

Rule these slaves with me Judah! As brothers under Rome. Like Romulus and Remus under the Roman she-wolf! Suckling at her great glistening teat!

SARA Goodness!

ESTHER No no Judah! Not slaves Judah! They are your PEOPLE!

MESSALA What?! What did you say?! SHE CAN'T TALK TO YOU LIKE THAT!!! Deal with her Judah! Do something Judah!

JUDAH *hesitates.*

ESTHER Yes Judah! What will you do Judah? Which side are you on Judah? The people or the masters?

JUDAH I've never really – I mean –

ESTHER Do you love me Judah?!

SARA and MESSALA *(Gasp!)*

JUDAH Do I – well I – um –

ESTHER Last night you say I love you!

SARA and MESSALA *(Gasp!)*

ESTHER I want to marry you!

SARA and MESSALA *(Gasp!)*

MESSALA Love her?! Marry her?! Is that what you want?

JUDAH Um –

ESTHER What do you mean um?!

SARA Esther my dear – we're very fond of you – we've known you for – well since you were a child – I mean –

ESTHER Well Judah?!

JUDAH It's just – well – rather – complicated, I mean, what would we do at the reception? Would you be on the top table with me? Or serving the food?

MESSALA MARRY A SLAVE JUDAH?!

SARA – you're a – sweet girl of course and you make wonderful falafels –

MESSALA Marry HER?!

SARA – and the best chopped liver this side of Joppa but frankly –

MESSALA Tell me you don't mean it Judah!

ESTHER Tell me you do Judah!!!

SARA – Judah really has to marry someone, I mean, you know – of his own – well –

MESSALA That's why I came back!

SARA – class really.

MESSALA For you Judah!

SARA Don't you Judah?

MESSALA I love you Judah!

JUDAH, SARA and MESSALA *(Gasp!)*

MESSALA And you feel the same. Don't you Judah?! DON'T YOU JUDAH?!

Agonised pause. **JUDAH** *stares at* **MESSALA.**

JUDAH Not really no. Sorry.

MESSALA *freezes. No one moves.* **SARA** *picks up the tray.*

SARA Chicken Messala?

MESSALA *grabs the tray from* **SARA,** *turns it upside down.*

The prop food is stuck to the tray so nothing falls. **JUDAH,**
SARA *and* **ESTHER** *gasp as if it has.* **MESSALA** *thrusts
the tray at* **ESTHER.** *They all gasp again.* **ESTHER** *runs
out with the tray.*

MESSALA The new governor is marching into Jerusalem in
a moment. I must immediately be by his side as is his
command. Thank you for the lunch Lady Hur which I must
hereby decline.

JUDAH Messala –

He marches to the door. Turns.

MESSALA I will never ever forgive you for this Judah! Do you
hear me? Never! NEVER!!! HAIL CAESAR!

Music:

*He bashes his breastplate. Turns and exits through the
door. He slams it on his plume which gets jammed.*

Music: *cuts.*

TIRZAH *skips in in a white frock.*

TIRZAH Don't worry if you don't like it! I won't be at all offen –

Looks round.

Messala? Where's Messala?

SARA Messala's gone my darling.

TIRZAH Gone?! When's he coming back?!

JUDAH Never Tirzah.

TIRZAH But he was going to marry me. That's why he came back!

JUDAH He came back for me Tirzah.

TIRZAH No no no he didn't!

JUDAH Yes yes Tirzah he did!!!

TIRZAH Oh it's always you isn't it Judah!

Jabbing him on the chest.

You you you you!!!

JUDAH (**DANIEL**) *(sotto)* Actually don't do that.

Sound effects: Roman legions.

TIRZAH Messala! Messala!

Runs to the parapet.

Look! There he is! There! There! Messala! Messala!

JUDAH No no Tirzah! Tirzah! Tis too late Tirzah!

He pulls her back. They grapple on the parapet.

TIRZAH No it's not! It's not! Not too late! Messala! Messala!

SARA The tile! Careful of the tile! I TOLD YOU TO FIX IT
JUDAH!

JUDAH *(grappling with* **TIRZAH***)* Yes I know I know! I'M SORRY
I'M SORRY!

SARA Your father would have fixed it!

JUDAH YES I KNOW HE WOULD! I KNOW FATHER WOULD
HAVE FIXED IT!

TIRZAH *and* **JUDAH** *crash against the parapet. The tile
slips.* **JUDAH** *tries to grab it but in vain.*

Sound effects: cuts.

They gaze down as the tile drops in agonising silence.

Sound effects: smash!!! Sudden uproar of crowd. Horses whinny. Soldiers shout.

WE'VE KILLED THE GOVERNOR!

Music:

Sound effects: loud knocking on the door. Soldiers shouting: open up! Open up!

SARA Soldiers massing at our gates!

JUDAH Mother! Tirzah! Get inside quickly!

SARA Hurry Tirzah hurry!

> **SARA** *pushes* **TIRZAH** *out. Turns to* **JUDAH.**

Judah Judah!

JUDAH Hurry Mother hurry!

Sound effects: knocking and shouting.

> **SARA** *runs out.* **ESTHER** *charges on.*

ESTHER!

Music:

ESTHER *Why can't you say no to your mother?!*

JUDAH What?!

ESTHER Or do you agree with her? That I am still just a servant-girl? Or a slave! Is that what I am to you Judah? A slave?!

JUDAH No no! Of course not! Of course you're not!

Sound effects: knocking and shouting.

ESTHER Then tell her you love me! Tell me you love me! Tell me you'll marry me?!

JUDAH I do love you! I do want to marry you! I do! I do!

ESTHER Then tell your mother!

JUDAH Um – the thing is – this isn't quite the right –

Sound effects: knocking and shouting.

ESTHER It's never the right moment Judah!

Sound effects: knocking and shouting.

JUDAH No this really ISN'T the right –

ESTHER *(grabs him)* The wicked of the earth doth rise Judah! And you must leave your mother and be a man at last! Stop your gallivanting and buffing and FIGHT! Fight for your PEOPLE! And fight for ME!

JUDAH takes her passionately in his arms.

Say it Judah! Say what you FEEL! Break your chains Judah!

JUDAH I – I –

ESTHER Very well! If you will not break them, I will! GOODBYE JUDAH!

JUDAH Esther!!!

ESTHER bursts into tears. Marches to the door. The door bursts open. Enter MESSALA and CENTURION.

Messala! Thank goodness you're here! It was all a terrible accid –

MESSALA Centurion! Take that woman!!!

The CENTURION grabs ESTHER.

JUDAH WHAT?!

ESTHER NO!

MESSALA And this man! Arrest him!

The CENTURION *grabs* JUDAH.

JUDAH What?! But on what charge?

MESSALA Murder of the governor.

JUDAH MURDER?! Is he dead?! Did the tile hit him?

MESSALA No it didn't as it happens. It missed him entirely in fact.

JUDAH So all is well! Thank heavens!

MESSALA Not for you Judah! You have been found guilty of – TREASON!

JUDAH TREASON?!

MESSALA And are already condemnéd!

JUDAH Condemnéd!!! But it was not done purposefulully!

MESSALA I know it was not done purposefulully!

ESTHER Messala! I beg of thee –

MESSALA Quiet! *Slave Girl!* Take her Away!!!

CENTURION Yes sir! Right away sir!

ESTHER No no no!

JUDAH No no no!

CENTURION *drags* ESTHER *offstage.*

MESSALA Centurion!

CENTURION *runs back on.*

CENTURION Yessir?

MESSALA Chain this man immediately!

CENTURION Yessir!

The CENTURION *chains* JUDAH *who does a lot of painful chain acting.*

Sound effects: rattling chains.

EDGAR *(sotto)* Sorry I can't quite get it – it's a bit er – sorry –

DANIEL *(sotto)* No there! Put it on there. Not there. There! Ow! Right.

At last they get the chains on.

JUDAH Agggggghhhh!

TIRZAH *runs on.*

TIRZAH No no Messala! Messala! Spare him I beg of thee!

JUDAH No no Tirzah! Keep back! Keep back!

MESSALA And who are you?

TIRZAH I am – you know who I am! I am Tirzah. Your sister! Your future wi –

MESSALA Centurion! Take her away!

TIRZAH What?!

JUDAH No no Messala!

CENTURION Ha ha ha ha!

TIRZAH Messala! Messala!

CENTURION *drags* TIRZAH *off.* SARA *runs on.*

SARA Take me Messala! Take me instead Messala!

MESSALA Very well. Centurion?!

SARA *puts on helmet, becomes the centurion.*

CENTURION Yes sir?

MESSALA Take the mother!!!

CENTURION The mother? Yessir!

JUDAH No no! Not the mother! Not the mother!!!

ESTHER *runs back on.*

ESTHER Not the mother Messala! Take me instead! Take me!

CENTURION *takes off helmet, becomes* SARA.

SARA No no! Take me! Take me!

Enter TIRZAH.

TIRZAH No no! Take me instead! Take me!

EDGAR *and* CRYSTAL *tussle violently as the* CENTURION, SARA, ESTHER *and* TIRZAH.

ALL No no! Take me! Take me! Take the lot of us!

MESSALA Very well, in that case take the LOT of 'em!

CENTURION *(putting on helmet)* THE LOT OF 'EM?! VERY GOOD SIR! TAKE THE LOT OF 'EM!

JUDAH NO NO NO NOT THE LOT OF 'EM?!

MESSALA Yes the lot of you!

JUDAH But where will you take them?

MESSALA To the infamous Jerusalem garrison gaol known as the infamous Fortress of Antonia!

JUDAH The infamous Jerusalem garrison gaol known as the infamous Fortress of Antonia!!?? But that is the most infamous Antonia fortress in the entire gaol of the entire Jerusalem garrison!

MESSALA It certainly is! Centurion! Take them away! To the deepest dungeon in the entire infamous fortress.

CENTURION Deepest dungeon in the entire infamous fortress? Ha ha ha! Right you are sir! Come on you slaves! Never to see the light of day again! Ha ha ha!!!

CENTURION *drags off* TIRZAH, ESTHER *and* SARA, *still voicing* SARA.

SARA, TIRZAH, ESTHER *(voices into the distance)* Messala! Messala! Mercy! Mercy! Save us Judah! Save us!

JUDAH Let me accompanany them at least I beg of thee Messala!

MESSALA No no no Judah. Thou wilt not accompanany them! Thy fate will be quite different. As a Roman galley slave wilt thou end thou thine days!

JUDAH AS A ROMAN GALLEY SLAVE WILT THOU END MINE THOU THINE MINE DAYS?!

MESSALA YES!!! Centurion?!

CENTURION *back charges on. Exhausted.*

Take this man – TO THE GALLEYS!!!

CENTURION *grabs him. More agonising chains acting.*

JUDAH The galleys?! Messala! Soften thine heart! I beg of thee!

MESSALA Soften mine heart!?? What dost thou know of the HEART Judah?! And the House of Hur you ask? Did you ask?

JUDAH I didn't actually no.

MESSALA In that case I shall tell thee! The House of Hur shall be but an example, a monument as'twere, to all those who would disobey the might of Rome! T'will be the place the House of Hur – were. Ha ha ha! Board it up immediately!

Sound effects: hammering.

Music:

Oh and Judah?

Music *and sound effects: cut.*

Don't forget. Down Eros! Up Mars! Ha ha ha ha ha ha ha!

Music: continues.

4 Desert/Nazareth. Day.

Enter JUDAH *staggering beneath the burning sun. A*
cruel ROMAN SLAVE DRIVER *brutally lashes him with*
a prop whip.

Sound effects: whip lashes.

SLAVE DRIVER Faster faster you dog! Do you hear me!

JUDAH Aghh! No! Spare me! Spare me!

SLAVE DRIVER I don't think so slave! Ha ha ha!

They stagger round the stage. A village well appears.
MARY *enters.*

Right. Stop!!! Two minutes!

JUDAH *collapses. Panting with exhaustion.* MARY *gazes*
at him tenderly.

Tell me woman, where might I find a well of water whereby
I might slake mine thirst for mineself and mine horse.

JUDAH Water water!

SLAVE DRIVER Quiet slave!

He lashes him.

Sound effects: whip lashes.

MARY Certainly o Roman slave driver. Here is the water thou
desireth.

MARY *draws water from the well. She gives him a jug*
of water.

SLAVE DRIVER Thank you o woman.

He grabs the jug, drinks greedily.

MARY But what about thine prisoner who lieth in chains and is near parchéd unto death at thy feet. Should he not also partaketh of thy water also?

JUDAH Water water!

MARY Listen how he cries out.

JUDAH Water water!

MARY There he goes again.

SLAVE DRIVER Quiet you dog! You scum!

He lashes him.

Sound effects: whip lashes.

Music:

He gets nothin! Orders of the governor hisself!

JUDAH Aggghhh!

SLAVE DRIVER QUIET YOU!!! Did you hear me! You dog! You'll be sorry you was even –

Music:

Everyone looks up at the music and shields their eyes. **JESUS** *appears. White robe, long hair. He takes the jug from the* **SLAVE DRIVER.**

JESUS Thank you.

SLAVE DRIVER *(entranced)* Right. And who might you be young man – um – when you are – at – er – home?

MARY He is my beloved son.

She gazes lovingly at Jesus. He gazes lovingly back.

The village carpenter. General handyman, cabinet maker and joiner. There is nothing in the world he cannot join.

JESUS *turns to* **JUDAH** *and the* **SLAVE DRIVER.**

JESUS Hello.

SLAVE DRIVER Now listen here you. Um hello. I am – under strict –

JUDAH I thirst.

JESUS I know.

> **JESUS** *kneels. Gives* **JUDAH** *the water.* **JUDAH** *overawed.*

SLAVE DRIVER Well just – just – a bit then. Alright?

JUDAH Thank you.

JESUS No, thank *you.* Well I better be going now, I have a sideboard to finish.

SLAVE DRIVER Right back on the – er – road you! You – you –

> **JUDAH** *gets up, still gazing at* **JESUS**. **JESUS** *looks at the* **SLAVE DRIVER**. *The* **SLAVE DRIVER** *gazes back, mesmerised.*

– er – whoreson – cur! Don't mind me saying that?

JUDAH No no. You're just doing your job.

SLAVE DRIVER Just have to – er – sorry about this.

> *He lashes* **JUDAH** *half-heartedly. Still gazing at* **JESUS**.

Alright?

JUDAH Yes thank you.

SLAVE DRIVER Want to sit down or anything?

JUDAH No thank you.

SLAVE DRIVER Okay. Yaa! Yaa! Sorry. Sorry.

> *More half-hearted lashes.*

> *Sound effects: lashes out of sync.*

> **DANIEL** *and* **EDGAR** *notice but carry on.*

They exit.

Music*: climaxes/segues into: sound effects: howling wind into cracks of thunder.*

Music*:*

Over the music, a gauze sea cloth comes in. The company haul on the galley set noisily behind it. The gauze comes out, revealing:

5 Roman galley – rowing deck. Day.

JUDAH, *bearded and stripped to the waist, is hauling on a huge oar in time to the music. He sits next to* **CRYSTAL** *who is hauling too. She plays an* **ANCIENT SLAVE** *with a long Ben Gunn beard and wig. They are attached to dummy slaves all rowing on the same bench.*

Enter **CAPTAIN**. *He charges up and down, lashing them with his whip.*

Sound effects: whip lashes.

CAPTAIN Faster faster you scurvy dogs!!! Faster faster I say!

Music: fanfare.

Slaves! Slaves! Raisin oars!

JUDAH, *the* **ANCIENT SLAVE** *and dummies raise their oars. They hang panting.*

All hail Quintus Arrius, the latest admiral of the entire Roman fleet.

Music: Fanfare.

Enter **QUINTUS ARRIUS**.

Welcome to your mighty flagship o mighty admiral.

See the four hundred and twenty oaken blades of her mighty oars. One might call her – awesome!

QUINTUS ARRIUS Thank you captain. Now then –

CAPTAIN Slaves! Drop oars for the admiral's arrival!

JUDAH, *slave and dummies let oars go.*

Sound effects: splash!

Water thrown at **ARRIUS** *from offstage.*

CAPTAIN Sorry about that admiral.

QUINTUS ARRIUS Quite alright. Now I just want to say –

CAPTAIN Raisin oars! To listen to the admiral!

JUDAH, *slaves push on oars. The oars raise.*

QUINTUS ARRIUS Right. Er – stand easy men.

CAPTAIN Very good sir. Stand easy men.

JUDAH, *slave and dummies let oars go.*

Sound effects: splash!

Water thrown at ARRIUS *from offstage.*

CAPTAIN Sorry about that admiral.

QUINTUS ARRIUS Quite alright. Erm anyway just wanted to say –

CAPTAIN Raisin oars! Admiral speakin!

JUDAH, *slave etc push on oars.*

QUINTUS ARRIUS No no that won't be necessary captain.

CAPTAIN Right ye are sir. Drop your oars when the admiral tells you – you dogs!

JUDAH, *slave and dummies let oars go.*

Sound effects: splash!

Water thrown at ARRIUS *from offstage.*

Sorry about that admiral! Raisin oars!

QUINTUS ARRIUS Actually can we stop this now please?

CAPTAIN Stop it sir, right sir, thank you. DROP THOSE OARS YOU DOGS!

JUDAH, *slave and dummies let oars go.*

QUINTUS ARRIUS No – no – no.

Sound effects: splash!

Water thrown at ARRIUS *from offstage.* ARRIUS/EDGAR
sighs.

CAPTAIN Sorry sir.

QUINTUS ARRIUS Right captain?

CAPTAIN Yes sir?

QUINTUS ARRIUS I'll just examine the men if that's convenient.

CAPTAIN Examine the men sir? Very good sir.

QUINTUS ARRIUS *(Examines dummies biceps etc)* Very good.
Excellent. Splendid. Oh dear. This one doesn't look very
well – looks a little – er –

CAPTAIN Floppy sir?

QUINTUS ARRIUS Well dead actually.

CAPTAIN Gets 'em like that sir after a couple of years.

QUINTUS ARRIUS Right. And um –

Gazing at JUDAH.

– this one here? How long has he been – er –

CAPTAIN That one there sir? Four and a half years this one sir.

QUINTUS ARRIUS *Four and a half years?!*

CAPTAIN Finest rower on the vessel if you want to know admiral.
I seen his oar bend almost to breakin sir!

QUINTUS ARRIUS Really?

He gazes entranced at JUDAH. JUDAH *stares back.*

Something of a disconcerting and insolent look he hath.

CAPTAIN He doth indeed your highness. Stop staring at the
ambulance with your disconcertin and insolent look!!!

Runs up. Lashes JUDAH.

You dog! Bilge rat! Scurvy knave!

Sound effects: whip lashes.

QUINTUS ARRIUS Captain captain!

CAPTAIN *(lashing* **JUDAH***)* Yes sir?

QUINTUS ARRIUS That's enough captain.

CAPTAIN *(stops lashing)* Right sir. Thankee sir very good sir.

QUINTUS ARRIUS *(approaches* **JUDAH***)* So tell me – er –

CAPTAIN Stand up seventy-seven when the admiral's talkin!!!

JUDAH *stands.*

QUINTUS ARRIUS Right. Thank you captain. So um – seventy-seven, do you have a – er – name?

JUDAH*'s brow furrows.*

Music:

CAPTAIN Admiral sir! Scuse for speakin sir outta turn sir. But slaves has their names taken from 'em sir 'pon arival sir. It will have been entirely expunged from his mind sir.

QUINTUS ARRIUS Quite right captain. I knew that. I simply wanted to – um –

CAPTAIN But I tell ye somethin sir. Summat keeps this one alive sir and no mistake! Gawd knows what it is sir. Tis a mystery sir!

QUINTUS ARRIUS A mystery? How intriguing. So what ist keeps thee alive boy?

JUDAH What – ist – keeps – me –

CAPTAIN Keep your mouth shut ye scurvy dog! NO TALKIN ON DECK!!!

Music: *cuts.*

QUINTUS ARRIUS Actually captain on second thoughts I think perhaps I might speak with him privately in my private quarters.

CAPTAIN Privately in your private quarters your highness! But that is very much against –

QUINTUS ARRIUS Inmyprivatequarters!!! AmItheadmiraloramInot?!

CAPTAIN Your quarters my lord. Straight away sir thankoo sir!

Music:

6 The Ocean. Night.

A model Roman galley rows slowly across the horizon. A full moon rises. This is a headpiece worn and operated by CRYSTAL.

7 Admiral's quarters. Night.

Sound effects: waves lapping. Creaking of boat.

ARRIUS *is lying in a tiny hammock.*

JUDAH *enters.* **ARRIUS** *jumps with shock.*

QUINTUS ARRIUS Aggh! What do you want?

JUDAH You asked to see me.

QUINTUS ARRIUS Did I? Ah yes that's right. I did yes. Um – do come in.

ARRIUS gets up. JUDAH comes in. They are jammed very close together.

Sorry about the – erm – room. Rather cramped I'm afraid.

JUDAH Cabin.

QUINTUS ARRIUS Cabin! Right. Sorry. Still getting used to all this navy lark. Anyway it's home.

He chuckles nervously.

So what can I show you? Um – hammock.

They edge round each other.

Sorry.

JUDAH Sorry.

QUINTUS ARRIUS Rudimentary compass. Don't ask me how it works.

Opens porthole, **JUDAH** *looks out.*

Nice little porthole.

JUDAH Thank you.

QUINTUS ARRIUS Glass of sherry? Twiglet?

Gives him sherry and twiglet. JUDAH *wolfs them down.*

Another?

JUDAH *wolfs them down.*

Right. So erm good. So anyway – I happened to notice you're um – very very – well – you have an excellent you know – physique so to speak. Very fit clearly. So – do you – work out at all or –

JUDAH I'm a galley slave.

QUINTUS ARRIUS Right.

JUDAH Chained to an oar for four and a half years.

QUINTUS ARRIUS Course.

JUDAH Keeps me quite fit.

QUINTUS ARRIUS Absolutely. I can see. So – erm – how are you?

JUDAH Not very good really.

QUINTUS ARRIUS Quite. Well you wouldn't be. Not a lot of protein or greens on board I imagine. And the whipping can't help.

JUDAH It's hell.

QUINTUS ARRIUS Right. Quite. Anyway – well the thing is – I – well – I run a school for charioteers. Lots of horses and racing and - chariots and – er – men obviously. So just wondered if you'd done any chariot racing ever?

Something sparks in JUDAH'*s mind.*

Music:

JUDAH *(he pulls on imaginary reins)* Down Eros! Up Mars!

QUINTUS ARRIUS Sorry?

JUDAH *(mimes skidding rund a bend)* Down Eros! Up Mars!

QUINTUS ARRIUS Right! Marvellous! So – well if you – er – happened to fancy a bit of a whizz round the circus –

JUDAH Judah Ben Hur.

QUINTUS ARRIUS Judah Ben –

JUDAH My name.

QUINTUS ARRIUS Your name?

JUDAH Judah Ben Hur. Judah Ben HUR!!!

QUINTUS ARRIUS Judah Ben Hur?! Judah Ben Hur?! Not Judah Ben Hur the Prince of Hur of the house of Hur?! Son of Obadiah Hur? The famously rich, enormously powerful and mighty merchant Hur??!

JUDAH Yes!!!

QUINTUS ARRIUS But thy story has travelled to the very throne of the emperor himself. Thou tried to murder the Judean governor!

JUDAH I DIDST NOT!!!

Music: cuts.

T'was an accident! I was falsely charged! Or stitched up if you wish me to engage in the vernacular.

QUINTUS ARRIUS Stitched up?! In the vernacular?! Who didst such a thing to thee?

JUDAH MESSALA!!!

QUINTUS ARRIUS MESSALA?!

JUDAH You know him?!

QUINTUS ARRIUS I met him once at Meta Pontum! Never liked him!

JUDAH Aggggghhhhh!

QUINTUS ARRIUS What is it?! What is it?!

JUDAH The memories! The memories! In the depths of mine own inner ocean hast they layn buriéd. Now suddenly they all returneth with a vengeance! *(Gasps!)* I remember now! The gates of mine own home was sealéd!

QUINTUS ARRIUS Thine own home was sealéd?!

JUDAH My entire family blotted from the earth! Four and a half years in this filthy rotten stinking Roman rotting vessel! And never a whisper to tell me of their fate.

QUINTUS ARRIUS Who who?

JUDAH All the Hurs!

QUINTUS ARRIUS All the Hurs?

JUDAH My mother!

QUINTUS ARRIUS Lady Hur!

JUDAH My sister!

QUINTUS ARRIUS Miss Hur!

JUDAH Esther!

QUINTUS ARRIUS Est – hur!

JUDAH They could be –

QUINTUS ARRIUS Anywur!!!

JUDAH Exactly!

QUINTUS ARRIUS But WAIT! How knowest I thy story ist sooth?

JUDAH Sooth?! Thou knowest not what ist sooth and what ist not sooth. Only I know what sooth ist sooth and this ist sooth and sooth thist ist!

QUINTUS ARRIUS Right.

JUDAH *(falls to his knees)* Oh Quintus Quintus Quintus! Forgive me for my unexpectedly sudden forwardness but I beg of thee – I beg of thee –

QUINTUS ARRIUS What?! Tell me! Anything!

JUDAH Help me find them!!!

QUINTUS ARRIUS O dearest boy! Dearest sweetest boy!

Picks him up, holds him close.

– of course I'll help thee find them! I'll do everything in my power! I'll move heaven and earth! *I shall move Rome herself until we find them!*

(Sound effects: urgent knocking.)

But wait! What is that urgent knocking on my tiny cabin door?

The captain bursts in.

Music:

CAPTAIN *(searching for* ARRIUS*)* Admiral! Admiral!

Sees him.

Ah there you are! The Mesopotatomamanian sea pirates admiral!

QUINTUS ARRIUS The Mesopotatomamanian sea pirates?!

CAPTAIN Through the starboard porthole see my lord!

Open porthole. They all look through it. Bump into each other.

QUINTUS ARRIUS Sorry.

CAPTAIN Sorry.

JUDAH Sorry.

Sound effects: battle cries, trumpets etc.

QUINTUS ARRIUS Agggh! There they are! Look! Bearing down on Benvenutum!

CAPTAIN Bearing down on Benvenutum! What shall we do my liege? Prepare for battle immediately?

QUINTUS ARRIUS Right! Yes! Prepare for battle immediately!

CAPTAIN Prepare for battle immediately! Prepare for battle immediately!

VOICES and **JUDAH** Prepare for battle immediately!!! Prepare for battle immediately!!!

CAPTAIN But wait a minute! Whatchoo doin 'ere SEVENTY-SEVEN?! GED BACK TO YOUR OAR YOU WHORESON SCURVY DOG!!!

Pushes **JUDAH** *out.* **JUDAH** *exits.*

GUARDS! Chain up the slaves! Chain 'em to their oars! At the double!!!

QUINTUS ARRIUS Er sorry captain – er – what was that?

CAPTAIN Sorry sir?

QUINTUS ARRIUS Chain the slaves to their er –

CAPTAIN – oars sir!!! So they won't escape sir! Ha ha ha!!!

QUINTUS ARRIUS Right indeed captain. Very good! Ha ha ha! Can't have 'em escaping! Ha ha ha!!!

Suddenly stops him, whispers.

Captain?!

CAPTAIN *(whispers)* Yessir?!

QUINTUS ARRIUS Just one little thing before you go!

CAPTAIN One little thing before I go sir?

QUINTUS ARRIUS Listen – very carefully!

He whispers urgently to the **CAPTAIN**. *The* **CAPTAIN** *listens intensely, looks suddenly shocked.*

Sound effects: battle cries, trumpets etc. Louder.

8 Roman galley. Night.

JUDAH *back at his place.* OMAR *now voices and manipulates the dummy that becomes* SLAVE 2.

Sound effects: chains rattling.

ANCIENT SLAVE No no! Not the chains! Not the chains! No no! No no!

SLAVE 2 We're going to die! We're all going to die! No no! No no!

ANCIENT SLAVE Look seventy-seven! What is this I see?! Our chains are chained but thine is NOT!

SLAVE 2 Which means you can escape! And we can't!

ANCIENT SLAVE Who can have commanded such an highly unusual and unorthodox thing at the height of battle?

JUDAH I know not. But on my way here in the raging burning desert, newly a slave and parchéd at a well and near as I thought unto death – a similar thing occurred.

Music:

A boy – about mine age – did come unto me and didst give unto me a pitcher of water.

ANCIENT SLAVE A picture of water?

JUDAH *Pitcher* of water! *Pitcher!* Like a jug!

ANCIENT SLAVE Right.

JUDAH And my life was saved.

SLAVE 2 But why was it saved seventy-seven, why and for what purpose?

JUDAH I know not then. I knew not now. It is still a mystery.

*Sound effects/**music**: battle – resumes.*

ANCIENT SLAVE and **SLAVE 2** Oh no! But look! Look! They're coming! They're coming!

Sound effects: They're coming! They're coming! Save us! Save us!

CAPTAIN *(leaps up, lashing with his whip)* ROW YOU DOGS! ROW! ROW! ROW! Or you're all goin to die!!!

Music *and sound effects: cut abruptly.*

They all freeze.

Exit **DANIEL**. *He returns in his dressing gown to demonstrate the next sequence to the audience.* **CRYSTAL,** **OMAR** *and* **EDGAR** *assist like air stewards doing a pre-flight safety display.*

9 General stage/auditorium.

DANIEL Thank you. Thank you so much. And now ladies and gentlemen listen very carefully please as we briefly explain the next sequence. Kindly give us your full attention as any mishap at this stage could prove fatal. Thank you. For the first time ever on any stage – the Daniel Veil Theatre Collective are proud to present our meticulously researched and authentically awful Roman sea battle exactly as it would have been in the year AD 29. And in order to facilitate the historical accuracy of this re-enactment, we shall be attempting something unique and untested in the world of classical theatre. We shall be asking *you yourselves* to assist us in the simulation of an actual authentic Roman galley exactly as it would have been as it actually entered the bloody fray at the height of one of the most shockingly dangerous and violent sea battles in Roman history. And to do this we shall be asking you to actually row exactly as one would have rowed at the time. Thank you. So if we'd like to begin please by firstly miming the oars. I'll repeat that. Miming the oars. So if you'd take your oars in both hands.

Demonstrates with **CRYSTAL, OMAR** *and* **EDGAR.**

And now hold the oar up please! And you'll notice now you look remarkably similar to a herd of rabbits. So firstly, lean forward in your seats please and push the oar away. Now lean back. And pull the oar towards you.

EDGAR Push. Pull. Push. Pull. Push –

DANIEL Thank you Edgar. Very good. And stop please! Now then the people on the right or starboard are working much harder than the people on the left. Or port. Now this is all very well for you but not a lot of use for the boat which is now going in circles. We need to THRUST on the left. Lots more thrusting please! THRUST THRUST!!!

CAPTAIN *(runs up and down aisles whipping the audience)* Thrust you scum! Thrust! THRUST!!!

DANIEL Thank you captain. You see you can thrust if you want to! Now we turn to the people upstairs.

Or – as we call it – the gallery. Or in the Latin of course, the gallery. You are members of the Roman aristocracy. Hurling abuse at the galley slaves. Who are of course mainly left wing trouble-makers and poets and season-ticket holders and so forth. Now, for this sequence, we are going to break you up into three separate groups. Group A, Group B and of course Group C.

CRYSTAL *indicates the groups as air stewardess.*

And you will shout out one of the following historically authenticated abusive Roman comments. Group A. Your abusive Roman comment is: "ROW, ROW, YOU PHILISTINE SCUM!" Try it please. Rather conversational I thought. And again please. Much better! Now Group B. "HA! HA! THAT'LL TEACH YOU TO HAVE DISSIDENT BELIEFS!" Now you've been at sea for nine months and you're also extremely bigoted! Try it AGAIN please. Marvellous! And finally Group C. "DO GET A SHIFT ON WITH THE ROWING, WE'VE GOT TO BE IN SYRACUSE BY TEA TIME!" All together please. That was very authentic. Now one more time with feeling. And now A, B and C all together! And go! So let us now return to the agonising world of the stinking galley slaves and hear their dreadful and heart-rending cries, many of which were actually made at the time. So number one, read from your card please?

AUDIENCE 1 Aaaagh!

DANIEL And slump over please. Good. Number two?

AUDIENCE 2 No more, no more, I beg of you!

DANIEL Thank you very much. Number three?

AUDIENCE 3 May your vineyards rot and your aqueducts crumble, you Roman dogs!

DANIEL Very moving. Number four please?

AUDIENCE 4 Oh shut up everyone, they're only doing their job!

DANIEL Not the most popular member of the crew. Number five?

AUDIENCE 5 Water!!! Water!!!

DANIEL Brilliant! Number six please?

AUDIENCE 6 Agghh! Erggh! Aggghh!

DANIEL Marvellous. And slump. Thank you. Number seven?

AUDIENCE 7 Stop stop! This is all too much! I can't go on!

DANIEL That was a Roman theatre critic. Number eight?

AUDIENCE 8 My manacles are hurting!

DANIEL Number nine?

AUDIENCE 9 You think you've got problems! You should see my rollocks!

DANIEL A little joke to amuse the galley slaves. Now then numbers one to nine in quick succession. And now even faster! Excellent. Now rowers are you ready? Oars in both hands! And ready with your desperate cries and abusive phrases! And aristocrats standing by with your historically authenticated abusive phrases? Good! And row!

Music: battle/rowing – builds over this sequence.

The audience row! And shout!

FASTER! FASTER!!!

The **CAPTAIN** *runs up and down the theatre aisles, lashing with his whip.*

CAPTAIN FASTER! FASTER! YOU DOGS! YOU WHORESON FILTH! FASTER! FASTER! FASTER!

EDGAR Row! Row! You dogs! You scurvy scum!

Music: faster and faster.

DANIEL *shouts at them to go faster and shout louder. The* **CAPTAIN** *charges up and down, lashing and goading.*

Music: *climaxes.*

DANIEL And STOP!!! And oars up!!! And lets hear a big cheer please for our abusive Romans and authentic galley slaves!

Audience cheer and applaud.

10 Galley upper deck. Night.

Music: Battle cuts back in.

Enter CAPTAIN, *rushing in.*

CAPTAIN Admiral admiral sir! Look sir!!! They're ramming us sir!!!

JUDAH and ALL RAMMING US?! OH NO OH NO!!! WE'RE BEING RAMMED!!! AGGGHHH!!!

The prow of a pirate ship bursts on to the stage. Smoke pours in. ARRIUS, CAPTAIN *etc cry out in horror.*

Sound effects: shouting soldiers, dying slaves, cracking timbers, swords clashing, trumpets and bugles, screaming men, cracking timbers.

CAPTAIN They're boarding us, they're boarding us!!!

JUDAH Quick! Fight men, fight!!!

Pirate dummies are thrown on through the smoke. ARRIUS, JUDAH *etc fight off the dummies.* JUDAH/ DANIEL *and* CAPTAIN/OMAR *start an unrehearsed fight. They start to whack each other with dummies.* ESTHER *and* EDGAR *pull them apart and hurl the dummies into the audience.* EDGAR *becomes* ARRIUS *again and grabs a dummy. He wrestles with it. They lurch dangerously to the side of the boat.*

QUINTUS ARRIUS Judah – Judah! Aggggh!

ARRIUS *and the dummy fall into the sea.* JUDAH *sees them go. Shouts after them.*

JUDAH No no!!! Quintus, Quintus, Quintus Aaaaaaaa –

He leaps after him and freezes mid-leap on one leg. Turns to the audience.

DANIEL Just to say if any casting directors or producers or angels happen to be in tonight, the Daniel Veil Collective – and particularly myself obviously – will be delighted to meet any interested parties after the show. Not during the interval if you don't mind as we'll be unloading the chariots. Thank you.

Blackout.

Music*: climaxes*

End of Act One

ACT TWO

11 Pre-show.

Music:

DANIEL *enters in his dressing gown.*

Music: fades.

DANIEL Ladies and gentlemen, before we start act two of Ben Hur – A Tale of the Christ by General Lew Wallace – I'd like to say as artistic director of the Daniel Veil Theatre Collective that we all feel that the show is going very well. Sadly, however, I do have some rather disappointing news which I feel I should mention if we are to carry on. I have just this moment received a text from the member of my family who was due to attend this evening's world premiere performance and am informed by this person, at the last minute I might add, that there are leaves on the Metropolitan line apparently so delays are highly likely and it'll be a miracle if she makes it. This last minute change of heart is not untypical. It has gone on since I can remember but I did think that possibly this time –

Enter **CRYSTAL.**

(Surprised) Crystal Singer ladies and –

CRYSTAL *(sotto voce)* Chariots.

DANIEL Sorry?

CRYSTAL Chariots!

DANIEL Ah yes – right – um – unfortunately there is another piece of disappointing news – um – concerning the world-famous and iconic chariot race, which we've had to unfortunately – um –

CRYSTAL – cut –

DANIEL – right – um –

Clanking and bangs offstage. An electric drill. Voices offstage barely audible.

EDGAR *(offstage)* Omar! I wouldn't!

OMAR *(offstage)* What?

Exit CRYSTAL *hurriedly.*

CRYSTAL *(offstage)* Omar! Leave it!

DANIEL – we've got the chariots, we've er put them together, but they only just arrived and we don't quite know – how to use them, or if they're –

CRYSTAL *(offstage)* – safe.

DANIEL Right – or um –

EDGAR *(offstage)* – legal.

DANIEL Quite. However – we've er –

More clanking.

– thought on our feet and quickly re-rehearsed the entire sequence under my guidance and the chariot race will go ahead! In mime. And we're certain you won't be able to tell the difference. And so on with the –

Music: *resumes from Act One.*

Sound effects: screaming, fighting men. Breaking timbers. Crackling flames fade.

12 Raft. Open sea. Day.

JUDAH *and* ARRIUS *on a tossing raft. They cling to the mast.* ARRIUS *tries to leap off.* JUDAH *holds him back.*

QUINTUS ARRIUS No no no! Do not stop me!!! I am responsible for the greatest Roman defeat in Roman history! Tis my duty to die the Roman way! Oh! Why did you save me from the burning waves when I fell from the boat?!

JUDAH I saved YOU because you saved ME!

QUINTUS ARRIUS That's right I did! But now – tis to no avail! Toss me into the waves I beg of thee!

JUDAH Certainly not!

QUINTUS ARRIUS In that case let me toss myself off!

JUDAH I'd really rather you didn't! But wait!

Suddenly spots something.

What is that I see?!

Gasps!

A sail I see upon the distant horizon!

QUINTUS ARRIUS A sail you see upon the distant horizon? What kind of sail on the distant horizon? Not – not – A ROMAN SAIL?!

JUDAH YES! A ROMAN SAIL!!!

QUINTUS ARRIUS Aghhhh! In that case we are doomed! Hemlock for me! Rollocks for you!

The prow of a galley enters.

There is no escape! I must accept my fate!

A HELMETED CAPTAIN *appears on the prow.*

HELMETED CAPTAIN Ahoy there! Is that the admiral Arrius admiral of the Roman fleet?

QUINTUS ARRIUS Might be.

HELMETED CAPTAIN Admiral admiral! I have news news!

QUINTUS ARRIUS News news? Tell me captain. I brace myself to hear it.

HELMETED CAPTAIN Brace not my liege. A mighty and resounding victory is thine!

QUINTUS ARRIUS *(amazed)* Victory?! Victory?! But how canst this be might I ask?!

HELMETED CAPTAIN The merciless Mesopotatomamanian sea pirates are all routed! And the emperor hails thee saviour of Rome!

QUINTUS ARRIUS Saviour of Rome?! Saviour of Rome?! Then in that case not only should I be hailed saviour of Rome but this young man also should be hailed saviour of Rome also!

HELMETED CAPTAIN A Slave?! Slaviour of Rome?! Ha ha ha ha ha!

QUINTUS ARRIUS A slave no more captain! Now a Roman!

JUDAH Me a Roman?! But – but –

QUINTUS ARRIUS No buts Judah! To Rome we go and – to Rome – we go!

He leaps off the raft and exits, making it spring back violently. **DANIEL** *falls on the stage. Scrambles awkwardly back on to the raft.* **EDGAR** *runs back on.*

EDGAR Sorry! Sorry!

Tries to push the raft off.

DANIEL *(sotto)* NOT YET, NOT YET!

HELMETED CAPTAIN Sound the salute!

Music: fanfare.

FIRE!

A large cannon appears on the prow. The barrel tilts up.

Sound effects: loud cannon fire.

A puff of smoke. A tiny cannon ball drops out.

Music:

JUDAH *stands heroically on the raft, leaving* **EDGAR** *to push it offstage.* **EDGAR** *staggers beneath the weight.* **CRYSTAL** *comes on to help him. She glares at* **DANIEL.** *Meanwhile* **OMAR** *hefts off the galley. This is also very unwieldy and heavy. They all glare at* **DANIEL** *as they shove raft and galley noisily into the wings.* **DANIEL** *glides off in heroic pose. The mists of time fill the stage.*

Enter **GENERAL LEW.** *Pulling on his uniform. Barely recovered from his naval exertions. He finds his way through the smoke.*

GENERAL LEW Well well howdy there again dear audience. And so – since that fateful day after the battle – we move on one year more in our tale and lo! The fortunes of Judah Ben Hur hath changeth yet again and a whole new world hath doth opened up unto him. The world of Ancient Rome!

Music:

The company haul on Ancient Rome. Roman pillars, vases of decadent feathers and flowers and a naked statue of the Venus de Milo.

And now let us raise a new curtain on our drama on a night of exotic Roman no holds barred decadence.

Music: exotic dance.

GENERAL LEW *exits through the smoke.*

13 Villa of Arrius. Night.

DANIEL, **CRYSTAL** *and* **OMAR** *enter. They perform a traditional sand dance eg Wilson, Betty and Keppel.*

They bow and exeunt.

Sound effects: applause.

Enter **QUINTUS ARRIUS** – *only just changed from* **GENERAL LEW** *into his toga.*

QUINTUS ARRIUS Thank you thank you. And thank you to our delightful troupe of nearly nude nubile Nubians! And now dear friends, Romans and...countrymen, welcome to yet another decadent feast hosted by myself Quintus Arrius. Newly elected consul of Rome, darling of the senate and friend to the emperor.

Sound effects: applause.

Thank you thank you. But wait! I know that trumpet!

Sound effects: fanfare.

Tis Judah Ben Hur! Who – since his arrival in Rome but one year ago – hath been gladly shone upon by the goodly goddess of fortune. In rapid succession he hath become – a) a citizen of Rome –

Sound effects: applause.

b) the champion charioteer of the Roman arena –

Sound effects: applause.

– and three – and most important – my adopted son and heir! Quintus Arrius the Second. Or the QA2.

Sound effects: Applause.

Enter **JUDAH** *in laurel leaves and toga. He and* **ARRIUS** *have a manly hug.*

Ah Judah Judah! Or should I say Quintus Quintus! Welcome home to our lovely luxury Roman villa. But wait till you see what fabulous new exotic Roman no holds barred entertainments I have for you tonight!

JUDAH Thank you Father. But Father?

QUINTUS ARRIUS Yes?

JUDAH I hope you don't mind my asking on such a Roman holiday – but is there perhaps – another purpose for all these fabulous nightly no holds barred exotic Roman entertainments?

QUINTUS ARRIUS Another purpose for all these fabulously twice nightly no holds barreds erotic Roman entertainments? But what other purpose could there be?

JUDAH They're not – diversions merely?

QUINTUS ARRIUS *(guiltily starts)* Diversions?!

JUDAH To keep me in Rome? To make me – forget?

QUINTUS ARRIUS Forget? Forget what?

JUDAH Forget – forget my –

He forgets.

I forget! Something I mustn't forget! What mustn't I forget? I forget! Ah yes! Now I remember! My past! That's what it is! Thank goodness I remembered. I must not forget my past!

QUINTUS ARRIUS Your past! Of course you must not forget my past! Your past! Why would I wish you to do that my darling boy?! But wait! Who is this?

Music: erotic flamenco.

CATALINYA *enters. A beautiful Carthaginian girl.*

Look! An exotic new divers – party guest! Who on earth can she be I wonder?

CATALINYA *approaches Judah. She stands very close.*

CATALINYA Hello.

JUDAH Hello.

CATALINYA You do not know me but I am a great admirer of your charioteering work.

JUDAH Thank you.

QUINTUS ARRIUS I'll just – rustle up some more oysters.

He exits.

CATALINYA I am Catalinya. From Carthagenya. Which will become known as Espania. I was born in the city of Barthino. Which will become known in years to come as Barthelona.

JUDAH Really?

CATALINYA Yeth. Yes. I also like to ride. Bareback. The wind in my hair! The pounding of the hooves! My castanets clacking in the wind! But enough of this cheeky chit-chat! Perhaps a little –

Looks into his eyes.

Carthagenyan cocktail?

JUDAH Sorry?

CATALINYA Carthagenyan cocktail?

JUDAH Thank you very much.

CATALINYA Then I shall summon my Carthagenyan cocktail waiter –

Claps her hands.

Valentinio!

Enter **OMAR** *as* **VALENTINIO.** *He carries a tray with two exotic cocktails. He is bare-chested and wears a somewhat figure-hugging gold loin cloth.* **DANIEL** *was not expecting the loin cloth. Neither was* **CRYSTAL.**

Ah! Thank you Valentinio! This is –

Strokes his chest.

– Valentinio.

JUDAH So I see.

VALENTINIO Hello.

JUDAH Hello.

VALENTINIO *(moves closer)* Hello again.

JUDAH Hello.

VALENTINIO *spins round, faces* **CATALINYA** *body to body. Breathing heavily, they gaze into one another's faces.* **DANIEL** *disconcerted.*

Music: wild dance.

CATALINYA *and* **VALENTINIO** *launch into a frenzied Apache dance.*

They hurl each other about with the tray of cocktails. Then grab **JUDAH** *and hurl him about too. The more he is hurled about, the dizzier and more aroused he gets. At the climax,* **CATALINYA** *pushes* **VALENTINIO** *to the floor.* **VALENTINIO** *pulls her on top of him. She pulls* **JUDAH** *on top of both of them. The breasts of the Venus de Milo spray over them.* **CATALINYA** *and* **VALENTINIO** *bathe orgiastically in the fountain and push* **JUDAH** *violently from one to the other. This has not quite been rehearsed and* **DANIEL** *is bewildered by* **CRYSTAL** *and* **OMAR**'s *well-rehearsed routine.* **VALENTINIO** *jumps up and leaps away with the cocktails.* **CATALINYA** *jumps up too and pulls* **JUDAH** *with her. She takes him in her arms* *and twines herself around him, breathing passionately into his face.*

Music*: yearning.*

CATALINYA O Quintus Quintus Quintus!

JUDAH O yes yes yes?!

CATALINYA Let go of the past!

JUDAH Let go of the past!

CATALINYA The past is no more!

JUDAH The past is no more!

CATALINYA Embrace the future Quintus!

JUDAH Embrace the future Quintus!

She spins him to face the front. They gaze ahead of them. VALENTINIO *wafts them with an Oriental fan.* CATALINYA'*s hair flies behind her.*

CATALINYA There is your future Quintus! Rome!

JUDAH Rome!

CATALINYA Or Roma!

JUDAH Sorry?

CATALINYA Roma! Spread before thee like a willing wanton woman.

JUDAH Willing wanton woman!

CATALINYA Gaze upon her Quintus!

JUDAH Yes!

CATALINYA Up here!

JUDAH Yes!

CATALINYA Upon the parapet!

JUDAH Yes! Sorry?

Music: cuts.

CATALINYA What?

JUDAH Upon the what?

CATALINYA The parapet. The – exotic ornamental parapet.

Music:

JUDAH Parapet? Exotic ornamental parapet?! PARAPET?!

CATALINYA What?!

JUDAH The tile! Don't touch the tile!!!

CATALINYA Tile?!

JUDAH The tile! Look! The tile! LOOK!!!

They all look down. Gasp at the height.

Don't touch it!

CATALINYA I'm not touching it. Valentinio?

VALENTINIO Yes?

CATALINYA Are you touching it?

VALENTINIO I'm not touching it.

CATALINYA We're not touching it!

JUDAH I should have fixed it! My father would have fixed it! He was a real man! Do you hear me!!!

CATALINYA Father?! Man?! Fix?! Hear?! Me?! Tile?! What are you talking about Quintus?!

Twining round him.

Come on baby! Relax! Relax Quintus! Valentinio! More wine!

VALENTINIO *exits through the curtain.*

Come Quintus come! You know you want to Quintus!

They embrace passionately. Disappear behind a pillar.
They reappear still embracing. But now CATALINYA *is*
TIRZAH.

JUDAH   Tirzah!

TIRZAH   Judah! Don't stop me Judah! Messala Messala!

JUDAH   No Tirzah no! Don't do it Tirzah!

> TIRZAH *disappears behind the pillar.* JUDAH *pulls her*
> *back. Now she is* CATALINYA.

Catalinya!

CATALINYA   Tirzah?! Who is this Tirzah?

SARA   *(offstage)* Judah! Tirzah!

JUDAH   Mother!!! Lady Hur!!!

CATALINYA   Who is that?!

JUDAH   Tis Hur indoors!

CATALINYA   Aggghh!

> CATALINYA *disappears behind the pillar.* JUDAH *pulls*
> *her back. Now she is* ESTHER.

JUDAH   Esther!

ESTHER   Judah Judah! Tell me you love me!

JUDAH   Oh I do love you! I do! It's just all so complicated with
Mother!

ESTHER   Aggghh!!!

JUDAH   Esther!!!

> ESTHER *disappears behind the pillar.* JUDAH *pulls her*
> *back. Now she's* CATALINYA *but in a Roman helmet.*

CATALINYA   Quintus Quintus!

JUDAH   Catalinya!!!

He sees the helmet.

Edgar!

CATALINYA What?

JUDAH Helmet!

He pushes her out.

EDGAR *(offstage)* Sorry sorry. It's pitch black back in here.

CATALINYA *reappears in the right wig.*

JUDAH *Catalinya?!*

CATALINYA Yes! Catalinya! Your new lover!

JUDAH No no! I don't want you! I want – Esther!

CATALINYA Esther?! Who is Esther?! You don't love Esther! You love ME!!!

JUDAH No I don't love you! I love Esther! I've always loved Esther!

CATALINYA *(shouting into the wings)* Quintus Arrius! Quintus Arrius!!!

JUDAH Quintus Arrius? Yes! YES! I nearly forgot! Quintus Arrius! He was meant to be helping me find them!!! QUINTUS ARRIUS!

CATALINYA QUINTUS ARRIUS!!!

QUINTUS ARRIUS *rushes back on, only just out of* SARA *costume.*

QUINTUS ARRIUS What is it? What is it?

CATALINYA We have a little – problem.

JUDAH WHERE ARE THEY?! WHERE ARE THEY?!

QUINTUS ARRIUS I told you to attend to his every –

CATALINYA I did attend to his every.

QUINTUS ARRIUS Quintus! My precious boy! What is it?! Who are you talking about?

JUDAH You know who! Tirzah my sister. Sara my mother. Esther my – Esther. We were torn apart by fates's fickle finger! Where are they?!

QUINTUS ARRIUS Fickle Fate's fickle fickle finger?

JUDAH You said you'd find them!

QUINTUS ARRIUS (*to* **CATALINYA**) Leave us immediately! And don't slam the curtain!

CATALINYA *storms out.*

JUDAH You said you'd do everything in your power to find them! You'd move heaven and earth! YOU'D MOVE ROME HERSELF UNTIL WE FOUND THEM!

QUINTUS ARRIUS Did I say that? Oh yes that's right I – I – did say that. Um –

JUDAH Well?

QUINTUS ARRIUS Sorry?

JUDAH WELL?!

QUINTUS ARRIUS Well – I – I – asked – um – around – and – and – where did he put them again?

JUDAH Who?

QUINTUS ARRIUS Messala.

JUDAH I told you where he put them! In the infamous Jerusalem garrison gaol also known as the infamous Fortress of Antonia.

QUINTUS ARRIUS Heavens! Oh dear! That doesn't sound much fun. How long have they been there?

JUDAH How long have they – I don't know, I don't know! Um – er –

He counts up.

Two...three...five um – er...carry the one...um... (*Gasps!*) Six! Six and a half years!!!

QUINTUS ARRIUS SIX AND A HALF YEARS! Aghh! Quintus Quintus Quintus! NO ONE could survive six and a half *minutes* let alone six and a half YEARS in the impossibly infamous Tower of Antonia Fraser! It would be unthinkable Quintus! Unimaginable! INCONCEIVABLE!

JUDAH Agggghhh!

QUINTUS ARRIUS Now listen to me Quintus my boy. Without beating about my bush. Without mincing my – whatsits – your beloved family is no more my darling boy! Or to put it more delicately – DEAD! There can be no other explanation for their silence!

JUDAH Dead?! DEAD?! Agggh! Agggh! What have I been doing for the last year! ONE WHOLE YEAR! Living the life of Old Mother Riley up the Appian Way!

QUINTUS ARRIUS So easy to do!

Music:

JUDAH Right! In that case –

QUINTUS ARRIUS Yes?

JUDAH – if they are dead –

QUINTUS ARRIUS Exactly.

JUDAH If they are dead –

QUINTUS ARRIUS Tragic!

JUDAH – if they are dead –

QUINTUS ARRIUS Nothing more you can do!

JUDAH I will seek my revenge!!!

QUINTUS ARRIUS Very sad but – what?! Revenge?! Upon whom?

JUDAH Messala of course!

QUINTUS ARRIUS Messala?!

JUDAH I will find him! And destroy him! DESTROY MESSALA!

QUINTUS ARRIUS No no no! NOT MESSALA! *(takes him in his arms)* Forget him Quintus! That's all in the past now! Forget the past! Stay here! Stay with me!!! Anyway he's miles away!

JUDAH Who?

QUINTUS ARRIUS Messala!

JUDAH Where?

QUINTUS ARRIUS In Jerusalem. He's the new commander of the Roman garrison.

JUDAH Aggh!

QUINTUS ARRIUS Feared and hated across the empire. He spends his entire life tormenting the people and going to the great Circus Maximus! Endlessly winning the dreadful and iconic Jerusalem chariot race!

Music:

JUDAH *(suddenly excited)* Dreadful and iconic Jerusalem chariot race?! Chariot race?! ENDLESSLY WINNING?!

QUINTUS ARRIUS What?! No no no! I didn't say that! I mean I didn't *mean* that! Besides the dreadful and iconic Jerusalem chariot race is even more dreadful and dreadfully more iconic than even the dreadful and iconic Roman chariot race!

JUDAH *(beside himself)* Even MORE dreadful?! Even MORE iconic?!

QUINTUS ARRIUS And not only that Quintus!

JUDAH WHAT?!

QUINTUS ARRIUS There are no rules in the Jerusalem arena!

JUDAH NO RULES IN THE JERUSALEM ARENA?! Ha ha ha ha!!!

QUINTUS ARRIUS No no no Quintus Quintus! Not Jerusalem! Don't go to Jerusalem I beg of thee! All those riots and roadblocks and rebellions and falafels and artichokes!

JUDAH What care I for – artichokes! All I care about is HIM! I will find HIM! And be avenged upon HIM!

QUINTUS ARRIUS No no no Quintus! Find peace in thy heart! Forgiveness in thy soul!

JUDAH Peace?! Forgiveness?! HA! Only vengeance is in my soul!

QUINTUS ARRIUS No no no, not vengeance Quintus! Twill eat thee up I tell thee! As the worm doth eat the fruit! As the fruit doth – eat the worm! War will rage within thee Quintus and you won't be able to stop it!

JUDAH But I have no WISH to stop it Quintus! For I do not just DESIRE vengeance. Now I AM VENGEANCE!!! And cross the seven oceans will I – till I – find he who – I will I be – avenged upon! Messala will be mine! Down Eros! Up Mars!

Turns to **ARRIUS**, *drops tone.*

Father I have been too long a'basking been in complacent slumbers and must unwaken'd be to be whereso'er mine destiny doth leadeth –

QUINTUS ARRIUS Oh Quintus –

JUDAH I haven't quite –

QUINTUS ARRIUS Sorry.

JUDAH There is no other path now but mine own path whereon I now must on I now must now I in I on I tread on.

QUINTUS ARRIUS Oh Quintus, for a brief moment, I thought I had found a son. A son I might call mine own. But now I see now. Though ye are our sons and our daughters, ye are not our sons and daughters. Yet ye reside with us, ye doth not belong to us. We house thy bodies briefly yet thy souls are free. Free to –

JUDAH Ought to be – getting off actually.

QUINTUS ARRIUS Right. Sorry.

JUDAH Sorry.

QUINTUS ARRIUS So. Well.

JUDAH Right. Bye.

QUINTUS ARRIUS Bye.

They have an awkward hug. Get their togas caught.

Sorry.

JUDAH Sorry.

They try and extricate themselves.

Actually! You're on my – sorry –

QUINTUS ARRIUS Sorry –

They lose balance. Stagger across the stage. Fall against a pillar. The pillar wobbles and falls. Revealing behind the pillar:

CRYSTAL *and* **OMAR** *kissing.*

This is not expected or rehearsed. **DANIEL** *and* **EDGAR** *stare aghast.* **EDGAR** *hefts the pillar back to hide them.* **DANIEL** *hefts it back again.* **CRYSTAL** *and* **OMAR** *have vanished.* **DANIEL** *stunned, stares transfixed at the empty space, then into the wings. Storms stage right after* **CRYSTAL** *and* **OMAR.** **EDGAR** *grabs him.*

Quintus Quintus! QUINTUS!!!

JUDAH/DANIEL What? What?

QUINTUS ARRIUS You must leave immediately!

DANIEL Leave immediately? But – but –

QUINTUS ARRIUS You'll miss the boat!!!

DANIEL Boat?

QUINTUS ARRIUS It's the last quinquireme for months! Quick!
Catch the neap tide before it – neaps! Quick! Leave I say!
Leave!

ARRIUS *pushes him offstage left.* JUDAH *exits.*

Music:

14 The Ocean. Night.

Sound effects: howling wind at sea/thunder.

Light effects: flashes of lightning.

JUDAH *enters on the prow of the Roman galley, pushed across the stage by* **EDGAR***, exhausted and still in his toga.* **JUDAH** *pitches and tosses on the boat as it battles through a raging storm.*

Simultaneously the model Roman galley pitches and tosses in the opposite direction. The same headpiece as before, operated by **CRYSTAL***.*

As they pass, **DANIEL** *glares at* **CRYSTAL***,* **CRYSTAL** *stares resolutely ahead.*

Sound effects: crashing rocks. Smashing timbers.

Music*: climaxes.*

15 Judean coast. Day.

A rocky Judean landscape. In the distance a Judean mountain. **DANIEL** *enters as* **JUDAH**. *He stands in a daze. This is partly exhausted survivor acting but mainly the shock of having just caught* **CRYSTAL** *kissing* **OMAR**.

Sound effects: lapping waves, seagulls.

CRYSTAL *enters as* **NABOTH** *a young Judean boy.* **CRYSTAL** *is nervous not surprisingly.* **DANIEL** *stares stonily at her. He is not going to help her.*

NABOTH Hello sir.

JUDAH Yes?

NABOTH How might I help you please?

JUDAH Sorry?

NABOTH How might I help you please?

JUDAH How might – you – help me?

Nasty silence.

NABOTH My – name sir – since you ask is – Naboth. Friend and neighbour to Balthasar the wise man. The wisest wise man in all the world.

DANIEL says nothing. NABOTH looks off.

I look out for him. For soon he shall be joining me.

DANIEL says nothing.

But this land I hear you ask? Why this land we call the Holy Land.

Music:

DANIEL does nothing. **NABOTH** *gasps!*

But wait! Thou startst! Some distant painful memory stirs within thee unless I am much mistaken.

JUDAH Many memories in fact.

NABOTH Many melly menny menanies?

JUDAH Yes.

NABOTH But what light is this I see a'burning in thine eyes?

JUDAH This light a'burning in mine eyes? This light?! This light a'burnin?! Is the light of vengeance!

The BEN HUR *story and the actors' story begin to collide.* CRYSTAL *has no option but to carry on.*

NABOTH Vengeance? But – but – whom wouldst thou be avenged upon?

JUDAH Whom wouldst I be avenged upon?

NABOTH Yes.

JUDAH *I'll tell thee whom I wouldst be avenged upon. I wouldst be avenged upon –*

BALTHASAR *(offstage)* NABOTH!

NABOTH But look look, tis Balthasar! My ancient neighbour whom I didst speaketh of earlier. Balthasar the wise man!

Enter BALTHASAR *in his wise man's robes.*

BALTHASAR Yea verily. Tis me. Balthasar the wise. The wisest of the – three wise men. Many wise things dost I utter, most of them almost entirely forgettable but this that I am about to utter is without doubt the wisest. Yea verily, there is no greater truth than this!

They all wait for the great truth.

THE SHOW MUST GO ON!!!

They are all stunned that EDGAR *is saving the show.*

So Naboth, to cut to the chase, tell me quick, what wast thou speaking of with this gentleman?

NABOTH Um – we were –

BALTHASAR Did he just ask – what are we doing here?

NABOTH Ah! Yes. He did. Yes.

BALTHASAR By this great, highly holy highly mountain? Did he ask it?

Turns to JUDAH.

Did you ask it? Tell us now I beg of thee. Otherwise we shall all have to – go home. Won't we?

EDGAR *glares at* DANIEL. DANIEL *turns to* CRYSTAL. CRYSTAL *looks guilty but not sure why.* DANIEL *makes her suffer as long as he can before at last becoming* JUDAH BEN HUR *again in his best* BEN HUR *voice.*

JUDAH Yes! I did ask it!

NABOTH *(relieved)* He did ask it!

BALTHASAR He did ask it!

Music:

Then verily forthwith let us immediately without further or much ado tell thee why we are here! And for whom we waitest! Tell him Naboth!

NABOTH For HIM!

JUDAH For him?

BALTHASAR He whom we didst chance upon all those years ago. Me and my two antique brethren. In the desert wastes. In the dead of winter. Beneath a star. A little tiny infant child all a'swallowed –

JUDAH Swaddled –

BALTHASAR Swaddled. Upon his mother's breast. That night so long ago. Way back in – in – in Act One. And now am I returnéd alone with my youthful neighbour Naboth. Hoping against hope that he is returned. That it is truly HE!

JUDAH Who?

BALTHASAR The new young rabbi of course! The carpenter's son or preacher man.

JUDAH Son of a preacher man?

NABOTH Or shepherd some say. Or fisher of men.

JUDAH Shepherd? Fisherman's friend?

NABOTH Yea yea. Thou wilt know him by his lovely long hair and beard and lovely sandals doth he wear.

Music:

JUDAH *(a memory returns)* Yes! Lovely long hair. Lovely long... sandals.

Music:

(Clutches his head) Ahhhhh!

BALTHASAR But what is it young man?! Something disturbeth thee in thine mind's eye methinks.

Sound effects: clap of thunder and lightning.

Light effects: spot on:

MESSALA *appears riding in a pool of light. He rears up laughing cruelly.*

MESSALA Ha ha ha! Down Eros! Up Mars! Remember Judah? Remember?

JUDAH YES I REMEMBER! I REMEMBER! VENGEANCE MESSALA! VENGEANCE WILL BE MINE!

*This is uncomfortably close to the recent situation.
But it is a rehearsed scene and they have to continue.*
MESSALA *laughs cruelly and disappears.* EDGAR *carries
on regardless.*

Light effects: change.

Music: *cuts.*

BALTHASAR Young man young man! Soothe, soothe thy fevered
   brow! Come with us I beseech thee. Meet this young rabbi
   and maker of miracles.

Music:

JUDAH NO! No! Do not manacle me to thy minacle makers!
   For now I go upon another path to go.

BALTHASAR But where? Which path goest thou?

JUDAH To the circus!

NABOTH The circus? This is no time for performing elephants
   and human cannon balls!

JUDAH No! To the Circus Maximus in Jerusalem!

BALTHASAR and **NABOTH** *(gasp!)* CircusmaximusinJerusalem!!!

JUDAH Where I shall race with Messala! To the death!

NABOTH To the death?! With Messala?!

BALTHASAR But why? What harm hath he done thee?

JUDAH More harm than it is possible to say.

BALTHASAR That's quite a bit of harm.

JUDAH Yes. You could say that. Farewell!

He storms off. CRYSTAL *looks anxiously at* EDGAR.
Saved by:

Music:

Light effects: white light beams down.

OMAR *enters as* **JESUS.** *White robe, beard, long hair.*

DANIEL *freezes, overawed by the music and the sight of* **OMAR** *in full beard and Jesus outfit.*

JESUS Hello.

JUDAH Hello.

JESUS Sorry to – bother you. But would you have any – loaves and fishes? For the people.

    JUDAH/DANIEL *nonplussed.* **BALTHASAR** *jumps to.*

BALTHASAR Loaves and fishes! Loaves and fishes! For the people! Naboth Naboth! Loaves and fishes for the people! Hurry Naboth hurry!

NABOTH *(looking into his bag)* Loaves and fishes?! Loaves and fishes?! Loaves and fishes for the people?! Um –

    Delving deeper.

Ah yes! We do seem to have – er – ah! Yes!

    Counts.

Five loaves and –

    Counts.

– two fishes. As it happens. How many people approximately?

JESUS Five thousand.

    They all gasp!!!

NABOTH Five thousand!!! Five thousand!!! But that's – that's –

JESUS These will be quite sufficient, thank you. I'll bring back the bag.

NABOTH Thank you.

JESUS No, thank YOU.

JESUS *exits. They watch him leave.*

JUDAH But who WAS this man? I KNOW him! Where have I –

NABOTH But look there he is now look! See how he feedeth the multitude. Five thousand people all eating our lunch.

BALTHASAR And lo! They are all – filled!

They gasp!

NABOTH It is a miracle! And now look! Look!

A little puppet figure of Jesus appears on top of the mountain. His arms go up and down.

BALTHASAR High up on the mountain. Or mount. He's doing a sermon. He's doing a sermon on the mount.

EDGAR *– fascinated – approaches the model* JESUS *that he hasn't seen before.*

DANIEL *(sotto)* Too close, Edgar, too close!

EDGAR *steps back.*

Music:

NABOTH List! List what he sayeth!

JESUS DISTANT *(the words come and go)* Blessed...merciful... peace-makers...peace...forgiveness...

BALTHASAR Peace! Forgiveness! Such simple words yet the answer to all the world and all its pain!

JUDAH *(holding his head)* No no no!

BALTHASAR Young man! What is it? His words doth touchest thee I think.

JUDAH Touchest me?! Peace?! Forgiveness?! His words touchest nothing!

The rocky backdrop closes. **PUPPET JESUS** *disappears.*

Music: cuts.

See! What did I tell you? Nothing! Here today! Gone tomorrow!

He turns to go.

I have better things to do!

NABOTH Wait!

BALTHASAR Wait!

JUDAH Nay nay! Follow me not! I go to my doom no matter – what!

Exit **JUDAH**.

Music:

Light effects and scene change.

16 House of Hur (distressed/cobwebbed). Night.

Enter JUDAH. *Looks about him.*

JUDAH Lo! Tis the home of my ancestors. Or my – ancestral home. I am returned. How it haunteth me! All the memories. All the wealth and treasures of my past. All my family gold and silver. Long gone! Long gone silver! Nothing liveth here now but ghosts and spirits.

A shape flits across the stage.

But what was that?! A spirit?

The shape flits back again. JUDAH *gasps!*

Spirit! Come spirit! What spirit art thou?

The shape appears. Walks into the light. It is ESTHER.

Music: *haunting.*

Esther!

ESTHER Judah! I cannot believe it is you!

JUDAH Yes!

ESTHER I have spent the last six and a half years in terrible grief!

JUDAH Have you?

ESTHER Yes!

JUDAH Thy grief hath only increased thy beauty.

ESTHER Thank you.

JUDAH Oh Esther –

ESTHER Six and a half years! In the infamous fortress of Antonia! Deep in its darkest dungeon! Till I 'scaped!

JUDAH 'Scaped?!

ESTHER Yes!

JUDAH How did you 'scape?

ESTHER With the prison laundry I 'scaped.

JUDAH Do they have laundry in prison?

ESTHER Not a lot. But enough.

JUDAH Well done!

ESTHER Thank you.

JUDAH But – *(gasps!)*

ESTHER What?

JUDAH If THOU 'scapest from the infamous tower of the House of Fraser, then – where – are THEY?

ESTHER Who!?

JUDAH My mother Sara and my sister Tirzah! *(He stares transfixed)* AGGHH! I do not need to ask! For I see it writ upon thine beauteous yet haunted features. No no! Do not spare me! Do not speak! I know that they are – *(gasping)* NO MORE! Destroyed – by him! By Messala! And now I know where I must go! To the –

ESTHER Not the –

JUDAH Yes the – *(gasps!)* And don't forget – there are no rules in the arena!

Music:

ESTHER No no!!! Judah! Judah! Don't do it I beg of thee! I cannot bear to think of – thee – dying – all alone – in front of millions! Oh Judah Judah Judah!

JUDAH What what what?

ESTHER Could you do you think you could, could you possibly –

JUDAH What?

ESTHER Forgive him?

JUDAH *(gasps!)* Forgive him?! Forgive him?! FORGIVE HIM?!
Not now I know they are – DEAD!

ESTHER But – but if they were – say they were – not dead?

JUDAH Not dead?

ESTHER Not dead!

JUDAH But they are dead!

ESTHER But if they weren't?

JUDAH If they weren't, what?

ESTHER If they weren't, would you?

JUDAH Would I what?

ESTHER FORGIVE HIM!!!

JUDAH I might. Possibly. Yes!

ESTHER They're not dead!

Music:

JUDAH *(gasps!)* What?!

ESTHER They are alive!

JUDAH ALIVE?!

ESTHER ALIVE!!!

JUDAH OH!!!

ESTHER So that's alright then!

JUDAH Yes!

ESTHER Yes!

JUDAH So where are they?

ESTHER What?

JUDAH Where are they?

ESTHER Who?

JUDAH Sara my mother and Tirzah my sister?! Tell me Esther tell me immediately with all convenient speed!

ESTHER Um – well – they are a little bit – how do I put this? Um –

JUDAH What?

ESTHER – ill. Actually.

Music:

JUDAH Ill?! A little bit ill? What d'you mean a little bit ill?!

Shouts out.

MOTHER!!! TIRZAH!!! TIRZAH!!! MOTHER!!!

ESTHER No no Judah! Judah! They are not here. They are –

JUDAH WHERE?!

ESTHER – in the – in the –

JUDAH WHERE?!

ESTHER – Valley of – Valley of – Valley of Jehosophat!

Music:

JUDAH *(gasps!)* Valley of Jehosophatat? Valley of the Jellytotosophats! That is the valley of – NO NO NO NO NO! The Valley of – the Valley of –

ESTHER Judah please!

JUDAH – the LEPERS! THE VALLEY OF THE LEPERS!!! LEPERS!!!

Charges off.

MESSALA! MESSALA!

ESTHER Judah! Judah!

JUDAH *(stops)* What? What?

ESTHER There may be a way!

JUDAH A way? What way? There is no way! No way – josé! You know as well as I do lepers can never change their spots!

ESTHER No no Judah Judah! Listen please please! I have a plan!

JUDAH A plan! What plan!? What kind of plan?!

ESTHER You have heard of the new lovely young new lovely young preacher man?

Music:

JUDAH Preacher man?

ESTHER Or fisherman's friend? With his lovely long robes and long lovely hair and young lovely beard and long lovely bearded sandals?

JUDAH *starts!*

Verily thou knowest him. I can see it in thine eyes thou knowst him!

JUDAH No no! You can't, you can't! I don't know who you're talking about!

ESTHER Thou hast heard his message!

JUDAH Message? What message?!

ESTHER To make the world anew.

JUDAH A new what?

ESTHER A new world.

JUDAH Right.

ESTHER Essentially a Marxist humanist dialectic along the lines of compassion, creativity, liberation and ecological responsibility.

JUDAH Erm –

ESTHER Where the world is well and wise and good. And all our little tiny little piddling personal problems fade to nothing. And we look after each other. And care for each other. And love each other. And not constantly fret about ourselves all the time! Behold I see a new heaven and a new earth. A world of love and peace and forgiveness!

JUDAH *(remembering)* LOVE AND PEACE AND FORG –!

ESTHER And miracles Judah!

JUDAH AND MIR –!

ESTHER Judah! The lame he maketh to walk, the blind to see. Only the other day a woman with dropsy he totally cureth.

JUDAH What's dropsy?

ESTHER I've no idea. But listen Judah listen! We could ask him to help US! Ask him to heal THEM! Thy mother and thy sister, Sara and Tirzah! While we still have time!

JUDAH Yes! Yes!

Suddenly reverts.

No! No! No Esther!

Music:

No one can help us! No one can heal anyone.

We're all of us lost and alone in the black night of this darkling world. What was it you said to me? That terrible day so long ago over the falafels? The wicked of the earth doth rise Judah! We must destroy them! Before it's too late! Isn't that what you said!

ESTHER No! Yes! No! I did say that but no! Not destroy! That way we just go on and on destroying! Until the world destroys itself! Until there is nothing! Oh Judah! Let us find him Judah! To heal the broken world! To heal thy broken family!

JUDAH Heal my broken family! Yes!

ESTHER Before it is too late Judah!

JUDAH Yes! My broken family! My –

Becomes confused. Becomes **DANIEL.**

– heartless family!

ESTHER Er – yes!

JUDAH/DANIEL My heartless mother!

ESTHER/CRYSTAL Erm – no! What? Sara?

JUDAH/DANIEL Yes – Sara! Where is she?

ESTHER/CRYSTAL She's – um – not here! You know – where she is! She's in the – um – Valley of Jeso-phatti-photty-potty –

DANIEL *(hisses)* With her fancy man that's where she is! Gallivanting round Ruislip! Leaves on the line!

DANIEL *exits furiously.*

CRYSTAL/ESTHER *DAN – JUDAH!*

DANIEL *re-enters. He is* **JUDAH** *again.*

JUDAH Yes?

ESTHER Whither goest thou? What seekest thee so furiously?!

JUDAH Whither goest I? What seekest I so curiously?!

ESTHER Furiously.

JUDAH/DANIEL Furiously. The arena! That is what I seekest! And the DREADFUL ICONIC JERUSALEM CHARIOT RACE! The most dreadful iconic Jerusalem chariot race the theat – *world* has ever seen! Where I shall surely kill Omar-salla! Down Eros! Up Mars!

Exits furiously.

ESTHER No No Judah Judah Jud –

She rushes out shouting, drowned out by:

Music:

The Circus Maximus sign and assorted Roman statues fly in.

We hear bangs and clanking from backstage. And an escalating heated whispered argument. They talk over each other and only barely audibly.

CRYSTAL Daniel! Daniel! We are not using those contraptions!

DANIEL Actually we ARE actually!

OMAR They're only lawn mowers!

CRYSTAL They're a deathtrap!

Sound effects: electric drill.

Omar!!!

EDGAR Please be careful!

CRYSTAL We're miming them!

DANIEL We're not now actually!

OMAR Apparently we're not now!

CRYSTAL SOMEONE'S GOING TO GET KI –

DANIEL TOGA EDGAR!!!

Music:

17 Circus Maximus. Day.

Light effects: arena

EDGAR *enters in a fluster in his Pontius Pilate outfit.*
He steps onto the governor's podium.

Sound effects: sixty thousand boos.

Music: *fades.*

PILATE Thank you. Thank you. And welcome to the Circus Maximus in Jerusalem. With a record crowd of sixty thousand people!

Sound effects: sixty thousand cheers.

Thank you. My name is Pontius Pilate, the highly popular new governor of Judea. And – this is Mrs Pilate. My lovely wife. Or co-pilot.

He laughs. **CRYSTAL** *enters reluctantly as* **MRS PILATE.**

Sound effects: sixty thousand boos.

Unfortunately, Mrs Pilate isn't wild about chariot races, in fact the first time she saw one, she went out like a light.

Laughs. Waits for laugh. Silence.

Jolly good. Anyway – delighted to say that, apart from a pretty tedious trial later on, all pretty forgettable I'm sure, I have devoted the day to introduce the highlight of the Roman sporting year, the ironic –

MRS PILATE Iconic.

PILATE Iconic. Jerusalem chariot race!

Sound effects: sixty thousand cheers.

And so a jolly big warm welcome for our contestants please.

First the winner of the last six and a half years – very much the favourite – our very own commander of our splendid Roman garrison – and where would we be without it? – Messala Sextus Messala!

We hear the spluttering sound of a lawn mower motor being started.

Music:

Sound effects: sixty thousand boos.

MESSALA *enters on his chariot. He rides jerkily round the stage, trailing smoke. He bows flamboyantly to the crowds. He halts. His motor clanking and spluttering.*

Music: *cuts.*

And secondly a brand new newcomer to the event. Yes all the way from – well – here! We present Judah Ben Hur.

Second spluttering motor starts up.

Music:

Sound effects: sixty thousand cheers.

JUDAH *enters on his chariot. He also rides jerkily round the stage, trailing smoke and acknowledging the crowds. He halts, his motor clanking and spluttering.* **CRYSTAL** *and* **EDGAR** *watch with mounting terror.*

Music: *cuts.*

JUDAH *and* **MESSALA** *face each other, pulling aggressively on their reins. Jerking up and down on their spluttering, clanking, unrehearsed machines.*

Sound effects: clanking and spluttering.

Music: *drum roll and trumpets.*

MESSALA Well Judah! The moment of truth! At last!

JUDAH Yes Messala! The moment of truth.

MESSALA I swore I'd never forgive you all those years ago! And I still won't!

JUDAH YOU won't forgive ME?!

MESSALA NO!

JUDAH I won't forgive YOU!!! HA!!!

MESSALA Forgiveness?

JUDAH AND MESSALA HA!

PILATE ON YOUR MARKS!

MESSALA Down Eros!!!

PILATE GET SET!

JUDAH Up yours!!!

JUDAH and **MESSALA** HA!

Sound effects: deafening gun shot.

Music*: racing.*

Sound effects: roar of sixty thousand.

Light effects: lights flash.

The two contraptions hurtle off round the stage, **OMAR** *and* **DANIEL** *doing furious chariot acting.*

Background film: Footage of passing buildings and landscape.

The two chariots charge round once and they're neck and neck.

MRS PILATE *holds up signs for the audience eg "Cheer", "Boo", "Shocked gasp!", "Long emotional sigh".*

The chariots career round again, lurching dangerously, but still neck and neck. Suddenly **JUDAH***'s chariot judders, stalls and stops.*

Sound effects: crowd of sixty thousand roar and boo!

MESSALA *carries on going round.* **JUDAH** *tries to push his chariot which is now pouring with smoke.* **MRS PILATE** *runs to help. They can't push it.*

DANIEL Edgar! EDGAR!!!

EDGAR *(hesitates)*

DANIEL PUSH IT!

EDGAR *gets off the podium and helps* **DANIEL** *and* **CRYSTAL** *to push.* **MESSALA***'s chariot hurtles past them. He waves at the audience.*

MESSALA Ha ha ha ha ha ha!

Sound effects: crowd of sixty thousand roar and boo!

DANIEL *(pushing the chariot)* Don't force it! Don't –

EDGAR I'm not really meant to do any heavy –

DANIEL PUSH YOU OLD HAM!

EDGAR *and* **CRYSTAL** *are shocked at this. They shove violently. At last* **JUDAH***'s chariot shoots into the wings, dragging* **EDGAR** *with it.*

Sound effects: enormous smash offstage.

A cry from **EDGAR** *offstage.*

Sound effects: crowd of sixty thousand roar!

Smoke pours on to the stage. **CRYSTAL** *runs off, appears again with a fire-extinguisher. She runs into the other wing. We hear:*

sound effects: whoosh! Whoosh! Whoosh!!

MESSALA's *chariot shoots on again through the smoke.*

MESSALA Ha ha ha ha ha ha! What do you say now Judah?!

Sound effects: another roar and boo!

JUDAH *grabs* **MESSALA**'s *chariot and jumps on. They are now squashed into the same chariot. They fight frenziedly. Now it is* **DANIEL** *and* **OMAR** *fighting for real. The chariot stops, starts, heads towards a pillar.*

Sound effects: sixty thousand: "Kill kill kill kill!"

The chariot hits the pillar. The pillar hits another pillar. The pillar hits the Circus Maximus sign which drops dangerously. **DANIEL** *and* **OMAR** *turn the chariot round. Jump back on. The machinery clanks and splutters, smoke still pouring out. They career dangerously towards to the audience.*

Sound effects: another roar!

Sound effects: sixty thousand: "Kill kill kill kill!"

Background film: runs into **DANIEL**'s *holiday movies.*

CRYSTAL *grabs the careering chariot. In the nick of time, she turns it, shooting* **DANIEL** *and* **OMAR** *on to the stage.* **DANIEL** *scrambles up, grabs the chariot and pushes it at* **OMAR**. *The horses' hooves appear to trample over* **OMAR** *who howls with pain.* **DANIEL** *keeps pushing the chariot. The stage is full of smoke. We lose sight of* **OMAR**. **CRYSTAL** *runs off. The chariot and* **DANIEL** *career into the wing.*

Sound effects: enormous smash!!!

Sound effects: crowd roar!

Music:

Sound effects: offstage: fizzling, crackling noises.

Sound effects: sixty thousand: "Kill kill kill kill!"

Music:

Set: Circus Maximus flies out.

18 Ext. Jerusalem. Main square. Night.

JUDAH *staggers out of the smoke. His charioteer's outfit
is tattered.*

JUDAH Messala is no more! But twas not me who killed him.
No no twas his cruelly mistreated horses, beneath whose
hooves he fell. Slaves for all their horsey lives. Crazed were
they and not surprising living as slaves like they did.

Enter CRYSTAL. *She hisses in a barely audible whisper.*
DANIEL *plays* JUDAH *to the hilt.*

CRYSTAL Where is he?

JUDAH Ah Esther! See I have freed thee! For a slave thou wast
also. Tis writ upon thine face. How like a horse thou art!
Why the long –

CRYSTAL What have you done to him!

JUDAH Of whom dost thou speakest?

CRYSTAL Omar!!!

JUDAH Omar?! Who is this O –

CRYSTAL Omar!

Exits calling out.

Omar! Omar!!!

JUDAH Ah Esther! All thy woes are at an end!

She enters, runs across the stage and exits.

No more a slave thou art! For see!

Music:

Thou art...free. Free! Do you...see! Free as a...bird is...free —

CRYSTAL *enters again.*

CRYSTAL He's gone!

Music: cuts.

JUDAH *(Donald Wolfit)* GONE?!

CRYSTAL *turns to audience. Very shocked and muted.*

CRYSTAL Ladies and gentlemen, I'm sorry but we can't finish the play. As one of our actors, Omar Lord, appears to have –

DANIEL *(hissing)* Omar?!

CRYSTAL *(hissing)* Yes!

They carry on hissing. Like a lovers' private tiff. They vainly hope the audience won't notice.

DANIEL Omar?!

CRYSTAL YES!

DANIEL Was it always Omar was it?

CRYSTAL Daniel! Do you really want to do this right now?

DANIEL We are – going out actually!

CRYSTAL What?! We've been out – once! ONCE!

DANIEL So do you want to go out with me?

CRYSTAL No!!!

DANIEL You want to go out with Omar?

CRYSTAL NO!!! I don't want go out with anyone!

Remembers.

Edgar!

DANIEL Edgar?! You want to go out with –

CRYSTAL Where is he?! What have you done to Edgar?

DANIEL *(looks around)* Um –

CRYSTAL BRILLIANT DANIEL! YOU'VE DESTROYED THE SHOW, LOST TWO OF THE ACTORS AND WE'RE NOT EVEN THROUGH ACT TWO!

DANIEL I DID IT FOR YOU CRYSTAL! THE WHOLE SHOW! EVERYTHING!

CRYSTAL DANIEL –

DANIEL All those agents and angels I emailed! I organised the profit-share! Wrote the show! Directed it! READ THE FRIGGING BOOK!

CRYSTAL Daniel—

DANIEL ALL FOR YOU!

CRYSTAL DANIEL!!!

Enter **EDGAR** *as* **SARA**. *In leper costume.*

EDGAR Excuse me?

CRYSTAL and **DANIEL** EDGAR!

EDGAR Are we finishing this show or not?

> **CRYSTAL** *and* **DANIEL** *stare at* **EDGAR** *in shock and relief. They go straight back into the play.*

JUDAH Mother!

ESTHER Sara!

JUDAH Tis thee! Agh! Leprosy!

ESTHER Agh! Leprosy!

EDGAR Can you wait actually?

> **EDGAR** *pulls rubber bands over his face. They are meant to create the impression of leprosy.* **DANIEL** *and* **CRYSTAL** *watch fascinated as the rubber bands snap.*

ESTHER *(still in character)* Are you alright?

EDGAR Apart from a bruised rib.

The last rubber band snaps on.

ESTHER Agh! Leprosy!

JUDAH Leprosy!

They go back into an approximation of the play. It is more or less what **DANIEL** *wrote but they know that – without* **OMAR** *– there can be no glorious climactic ending so are having to wrap the play up as best they can, semi-rehearsed, semi-extemporised, hoping the audience won't notice.*

CRYSTAL But Tirzah! Where is Tirzah?

EDGAR *limps off and brings back a pirate dummy in a ragged* **TIRZAH** *costume. He snaps rubber bands on the dummy too.*

ESTHER Tirzah! Agh! Leprosy!

JUDAH Leprosy! Agh!

SARA Come no closer my son! We are still extremely poorly. Are we not my darling?

TIRZAH (**CRYSTAL**) Mmm mmm mmm.

SARA Sorry?

TIRZAH (**CRYSTAL**) Mmm mmm mmm.

SARA *(stroking the dummy)* There there! Shhh! Shhh!

JUDAH Mother, as you may have heard Messala was a'slain in the chariot race. Not by me but by his – crazy horses. I had hoped it might have been an epiphanous and redemptive moment but –

SARA It wasn't.

JUDAH No.

SARA We, on the other hand, escaped from the dreaded valley of –

JUDAH – Jessy – photty –

SARA Exactly. With Esther. Didn't we Esther?

Music:

ESTHER Yes. We did.

SARA She came for us at dead of night and took us from that dark and dreadful place – into the light. To find him! The fisherman's friend. That we might be healéd. And make all things well again. But – it was not to be. We were too late. Weren't we my darling?

Waits for TIRZAH.

Weren't we my darling?

TIRZAH (CRYSTAL) Mmmmm.

SARA We were all too late. And now he is gone. Dead and buriéd these past three days. And we shall never ever be healéd! So now to our cruel abodes and lives and – whatnot – we must return and suffer the slings and arrows that life doth hurleth at uth – us which we mutht – must humbly accept. Acthept. Accept.

Music: fades.

So what we longed for was not to be. Our story was not alright in the end. But sometimes stories sadly – just aren't. Sorry.

They stand in an unrehearsed tableau of grief.

Light effects: fade. Then cross fade into: dawn light.

19 Jesus's Tomb. Dawn.

Sound effects: dawn chorus.

Music:

OMAR *appears as* **JESUS.**

JESUS Hello.

Everyone gasps with shock.

ESTHER JESUS!

DANIEL We thought you had – gone from us.

JESUS I came back.

JUDAH Are you "alright"?

JESUS Well – it's been a bit of a journey frankly. Rather a rocky weekend you could say. Still, had to go through it.

JUDAH Why?

JESUS To forgive you.

DANIEL Me?

JESUS Yes.

DANIEL Forgive me for what exactly?

OMAR Well you have been a bit of an arse haven't you?

DANIEL Actually I – I –

OMAR/JESUS No you really have been an arse. A right proper pillock Daniel!

DANIEL I don't think Jesus would speak like that!

OMAR Yes he would! You nearly ruined the whole bloody show didn't you Daniel?!

CRYSTAL You did actually Daniel.

EDGAR You did actually.

TIRZAH (CRYSTAL) Mmm mmm mmm mmm mmm mmm [you did actually Daniel].

OMAR Bloody collective! Dictatorship more like! Always putting me down for being on daytime telly – what's wrong with daytime telly? And you did all this for her, did you? You did it for yourself man! And thought you'd get her into the bargain. And calling him an old ham! *And* he's got a cracked rib.

EDGAR Well it might be cracked. I'm not – not –

DANIEL Then why didn't you all – actually – just – just – LEAVE?!

OMAR I'll tell you why? Because –

DANIEL – I know I said I was getting in casting directors and angels! I don't know any casting directors! I don't know any angels! And bloody profit-share! There's nothing to share! I've been a fool! I've been a bloody –

OMAR – we love you.

DANIEL Sorry?

OMAR We love you.

DANIEL *takes this in. Looks at the others. Looks at* CRYSTAL.

DANIEL Crystal do you –?

CRYSTAL Well no. Not like –

OMAR Daniel man! Don't push it! We love you. All right? We love you.

DANIEL Thank you. Sorry. Thank you.

JESUS Right – so if I may – excuse me –

Steps back into the light. Adjust his wig.

Music builds ever more ethereal.

I forgive you. On behalf of – everyone here. I forgive you.
And – I forgive – the whole world actually –

DANIEL Right.

JESUS So it's not just you.

DANIEL Right.

JESUS Though you were pretty bad.

DANIEL Right.

JESUS I forgive them –

ESTHER For they know not –

JESUS My line actually.

ESTHER Sorry.

JESUS *(opens his arms)* – for they know not what they do.

He lowers his arms, sighs with relief that the weight of forgiveness is gone.

That's better. So anyway – er – better be on my way. Do
the old – ascension. You know. Don't know whether it'll
work but – give it a go. Miracles can happen so they say.
So they tell me. Quite often when you least expect 'em. So
anyway – all you got to do – basically – right?

All you gotta do – is listen to your own heart that's all.
Be nice to people. Learn to stand in their moccasins once
in a while. Does wonders. And stop blaming everyone for
everything. And don't take everything I say so literally!
Bloody maniacs half a you. Go to the *heart* of the words,
not the letter. Oh yes and sorry –

ALL What?

JESUS I forgot to bring back the bag. Sorry.

ALL It's fine. Honestly. Quite alright. We can buy another –

EDGAR They only cost 5p.

ALL Thank you Jesus.

JESUS No no. Thank *you*.

Music: builds.

*JESUS steps back. Suddenly **ESTHER** notices something. She looks at **SARA** and **TIRZAH**. She looks again. She double takes. Gasps! The rubber bands are gone.*

ESTHER Wait! Sara! Tirzah! Look! Look at you!!! You are – you are –

JUDAH Healed! You are healed!

They all gasp! Look at each other, hug each other, weeping and hugging, weeping with joy.

JUDAH (AND ALL) Mother! Tirzah! Mother! Tirzah! Esther! Mother! Tirzah! Esther! Tirzah! Mother! Tirzah! Esther! Mother!

JESUS/OMAR Er –

*He nods towards the gallery, **DANIEL** follows his look. He gazes into the rear circle. He peers through the darkness. Suddenly sees his mother who made it to Act Two. Daniel gasps in amazement.*

Music: Jerusalem – very slow build.

DANIEL Mother? Mum?! You came! But you texted, you said there were leaves on the – you said it was highly un – that – it would – take a mir –

They all turn to Jesus and gaze at him in utter astonishment.

JESUS Don't mention it.

Very slowly Jesus ascends into the flies.

Lights effects: a great golden sun rises behind him.

JUDAH, SARA and TIRZAH are bathed in golden sunlight. They all look at each other. They realise they have made it and the play is done and they are still in one piece and all is forgiven. And more to the point nothing went wrong. And if anything did go wrong, no one noticed.

They all look up at JESUS, mid-flight. They all wave.

ALL Bye Jesus. Thank you Jesus. Bye Jesus! Thank you! Thank you! Bye! Bye! Bye! Bye Jesus! Bye!!! Bye!!!

Music: Jerusalem – builds to climax.

JESUS smiles down.

The End

EPILOGUE

HOW I FELL IN LOVE WITH BEN HUR

Patrick Barlow

I was exactly ten when I fell in love with my first epic. It was Cecil B. de Mille's *The Ten Commandments* and it was the 3pm matinee at the Leicester Essoldo and my birthday treat. It was the day my life changed. And my creative course was set. While my birthday entourage of school chums yawned and squirmed around me, I sat utterly dumbstruck and spellbound for every one of the film's two hundred and nineteen minutes, thrilling to every plague, every flicker of the burning bush, every glint on Yul Brynner's bald head. When fifty thousand groaning slaves toiled under the burning desert sun hauling up a two-hundred-foot stone obelisk for the as yet unoccupied tomb of the Pharoah Seti I, there wasn't such a thing as computer-animated anything. That was a real (albeit plaster) obelisk in a real long-shot with fifty thousand real extras, all in real Hebrew slave costumes, all on the payroll.

The Ten Commandments became a permanent feature of my imagination. With my birthday money I went straight out to Cowlings for Records in Market Street and bought the exquisitely packaged 33 1/3 rpm soundtrack record with its portrait of Charlton Heston – my new hero – in silver wig pulling the ten commandments from the glowing red fire at the top of Mount Sinai. When no one was home, I would put the record on the portable Dansette gramophone and open the window and march about the garden in a selection of towels (bath, beach and tea), turning the goldfish pond into the Red Sea, a spindly crabapple tree into the burning bush and our two dogs (untrainable retriever and neurotic baldng terrier) into the flocks of Jethro.

The music was barely audible and Ratcliffe Road Leicester a far cry from the Egyptian wilderness but it was enough for me.

For a while anyway.

Deep in my heart, I wanted the experience all over again. I only had two years to wait.

I can see the poster still. The giant crumbling edifice comprising those two unforgettable words linked by the strangely floating hyphen with wild white horses racing chariots at their feet.

It was 1959. And *Ben Hur* had arrived in the movie world. It fulfilled a deep need in a lonely Leicester lad that I've never understood or been able to explain. With my personal god (still many years before his barmy rifle-toting gun-lobbying days) in the lead and thousands upon thousands of extras, and a Roman sea battle and a glitteringly seductive villain and a funny Welsh sheikh and a twenty-minute (twenty-minute!) chariot race and a love story that went on a bit and Jesus himself popping in every so often (I was heavily into Jesus), not to mention the entire crucifixion and a jaw-dropping miraculous healing from leprosy sequence at the end that I wept at at the time and still weep each time I see it.

By this time, we had replaced the Dansette with a small snazzy Bakelite Philips record player with a detachable speaker in the lid on an eight-foot cord. What magic! I could now put the Miklós Rósza soundtrack (in its gleaming yellow sleeve which I still have) on the turntable, then stretch the speaker tight as far as the fish pond, turn the Philips up to full, and race chariots, row galleys, march through Rome and follow Jesus to Golgotha to my heart's content.

But again that wasn't enough. Deep down, deep down, I had a dream that wouldn't leave me. Crazy of course and doomed to failure, but there all the same. The dream to mount Ben Hur all over again but made by ME!

It was then that I noticed something else on that great and glorious poster.

It said in rather small would-be ancient lettering: *A Tale of the Christ* by General Lew Wallace.

Who was this? I wondered. Who was this general called Lew? And what did he have to do with first-century Palestine and Roman sea battles, chariot races, scheming sheiks and wicked tribunes, not to mention Christ, sorry the Christ?

There was no internet in those days, but I combed through our twenty volume Home Encyclopedia and lo and behold – there he was. General Lewis Wallace. Illustrious Civil War general and later judge. Presiding over the trial of both Billy the Kid and John Wilkes Booth (assassin of Abraham Lincoln) no less. And also novelist. Of many illustrious, lengthy and tiny-printed tomes. *Cortez's Conquest of Mexico*, *The Prince of India*, *Why Constantinople Fell*, *The Wooing of Malkatoon* to name but a few. But, while these titles vanished without trace, his last and most lengthy work was an instant hit. *Ben Hur – A Tale of the Christ*, written in 1880, somehow touched a deep public nerve. It was an immediate bestseller and has never been out of print since. When I asked, no one had heard of it at the bigger bookshops, like the biggest and most unappealingly named Midland Educational (Leicester) Ltd but there was a tiny dusty Dickensian-type bookshop called Clarke and Satchell with windy dusty corridors and high dusty shelves in a backstreet near the Cathedral (near where they were to discover Richard III) that I (young intellectual that I was) used to lose myself in for many hours on end. And there it was I found it. A 1940s edition in a torn cover with two racing chariots. I'd like to say I pounced on it and devoured it at a sitting. Pounced on it yes, but it took me a full term and whole summer holiday toiling like a galley slave through its tortuous imitation Thackeray and Dickens, its tangled, agonising unedited nineteenth century tiny-printed prose. It wasn't the Charlton Heston/Steven Boyd movie with thunderstorm crucifixions and drowning men in burning galleys and twenty-five minute chariot races and sixty thousand extras (so it said in the brochure) but it was something.

It was the real thing.

By 1960, I had turned thirteen and was undergoing the first cruel privations of the English public school system, a school called

Uppingham, alma mater of Boris Karloff, Rick Stein, Stephen Fry and Donald Campbell, world water-speed champion, and model for the wonderful Lindsey Anderson movie *If*. The ritual beatings, the ice-cold corridors, the mock-army exercises, the horrors of the rugby scrum, the casual SS-style bullying were all part of my tender adolescence. By astonishing chance, this hell was relieved by a visionary and brilliant English master called Mr Braddy who introduced us to literature and theatre and art and Shakespeare and Ibsen and Chekhov and Arthur Miller and Shaw and O'Casey and insisted we read Kenneth Tynan every week in the Observer and was also director of plays who gave me a part in *King Lear* despite my having a crippling stutter and released, not to say revealed, the treasures of my imagination and thus almost certainly saved my life for which I am eternally grateful. He never knew about my copy of *Ben Hur: A Tale of the Christ* and most certainly would not have approved if he had known. All the same I kept it with me – my guilty pleasure – secreted in my tuck box and there it remained. No Dickens for sure with its punctuation-free purple biblical prose but there was something about the story, the sweep of it, the breadth of it, the sheer pain and passion of it, that would not let me alone, that haunted me then and haunts me still.

All I had to do – to sustain me through those bleak and lonely Colditz years on the Rutland flatlands – was to turn each bible-thin page and pore over each miniscule word and re-imagine every scene in my very own personal movie remake. This kept me going through the dark cold hours.

I wrote the start of that movie more times than I care to remember ("SYRIAN DESERT. NIGHT. The sound of camel hooves. Three splendidly attired kings appear. They look earnestly up at the stars...") but never ever got past baby Jesus.

Unsurprisingly, over the years, the dream of the P. Barlow Ben Hur movie faded.

Though I did keep the book.

Which I forgot about.

Until it returned in the strange way that childhood dreams return in later life.

After the unexpected (to me) success of *The 39 Steps* and the question "what next?" was raised, there it was again. Leaping into my mind's eye. Alive and glowing as ever it was when I first discovered it in the tiny dusty bookshop behind the cathedral. The battered book with its miniscule print and two torn chariots on the front hurtling round the Circus Maximus, thrilling the Roman crowds and thrilling me. It could rise again. Maybe fifty-five years later, maybe with no horses, no desert, no chariots, no Roman galleys, maybe with only four actors but still as real to me as when I was twelve.

I wrote the above three years ago for the programme at the beautiful Watermill Theatre in Newbury where the play was first put on. And later for the second version – which is this version (many rewrites later) – at the splendid Tricycle Theatre in North London. The play has performed so far to great critical success and wonderful audience response and I am truly grateful for the support of truly exceptional, talented and generous producers, directors, actors, designers, sound designers, and, by no means least, stage crews who have helped bring this success about. A theatrical four-person epic – dare I say – that old General Lew – and certainly the little lonely twelve-year-old in the garden with his untrained neurotic dogs and his mother's record-player with detachable lid – could never even have guessed at.

I hope in your hands General Lew's *Ben Hur* will keep on keeping 'em guessing into the unforeseeable future.

November 2016